St. Charles Public Library
St. Charles, IL 60174

W9-AWA-483

THE LAWS OF **CHARISMA**

THE LAWS OF **CHARISMA**

How to Captivate, Inspire, and

Influence for Maximum Success

Kurt W. Mortensen

AMERICAN MANAGEMENT ASSOCIATION

New York · Atlanta · Brussels · Chicago · Mexico City · San Francisco
Shanghai · Tokyo · Toronto · Washington, D.C.

Bulk discounts available. For details visit:
www.amacombooks.org/go/specialsales
Or contact special sales:
Phone: 800-250-5308
Email: specialsls@amanet.org
View all the Amacom titles at: www.amacombooks.org

This publication is designed to provide accurate and authoritative information in regard to the subject matter covered. It is sold with the understanding that the publisher is not engaged in rendering legal, accounting, or other professional service. If legal advice or other expert assistance is required, the services of a competent professional person should be sought.

Library of Congress Cataloging-in-Publication Data

Mortensen, Kurt W.
The laws of charisma : how to captivate, inspire, and influence for maximum success / Kurt W. Mortensen.
    p. cm.
Includes bibliographical references and index.
ISBN-13: 978-0-8144-1591-7
ISBN-10: 0-8144-1591-1
1. Charisma (Personality trait)   2. Success.   I. Title.
BF698.35.C45M67 2010
158.2—dc22

                                                              2010010063

© 2011 Kurt W. Mortensen.
All rights reserved.
Printed in the United States of America.

This publication may not be reproduced, stored in a retrieval system, or transmitted in whole or in part, in any form or by any means, electronic, mechanical, photocopying, recording, or otherwise, without the prior written permission of Amacom, a division of American Management Association, 1601 Broadway, New York, NY 10019

About AMA
American Management Association (www.amanet.org) is a world leader in talent development, advancing the skills of individuals to drive business success. Our mission is to support the goals of individuals and organizations through a complete range of products and services, including classroom and virtual seminars, webcasts, webinars, podcasts, conferences, corporate and government solutions, business books and research. AMA's approach to improving performance combines experiential learning—learning through doing—with opportunities for ongoing professional growth at every step of one's career journey.

Printing number

10 9 8 7 6 5 4 3 2 1

CONTENTS

v

3 0053 00927 4955

ACKNOWLEDGMENTS

My grateful acknowledgments go out to all the people who helped make *Laws of Charisma* a reality.

I want to express my love and appreciation to my loving wife Denita and to my children (Brooke, Mitchell, Bailey, and Madison), for their love and support throughout this project.

I especially want to express special sweeping thanks to all my customers and clients who made this research possible.

I appreciate all my colleagues, parents, friends, teachers, examples, and associates who helped me along the way.

INTRODUCTION

FABLE: THE ANGRY BEE

After a long brutal winter, it finally happens—a beautiful warm spring day. You go outside and feel the warmth of the sun on your face and your body, and you take a whiff of the fresh air. You decide you are done with winter and want to let the warm spring air into your home. You open all the doors and all the windows. You feel the fresh air rush in and revitalize and renew your home. Warm air isn't the only thing rushing into your home; you hear the buzz of an insect. Out of the corner of your eye, you see a bee flying around your home. The bee seems so helpless that you decide to help. You want to show the bee the way to freedom. The bee keeps slamming into and bouncing off the large pane window in your living room. You open up the front screen door and try to direct the bee with your hands to safety and security. The more you try, the more irritated the bee gets. You're puzzled at the bee's anger. You think to yourself, "I'm only trying to save the bee's life." You finally try to direct the bee from the window to the open door by using your whole body. The bee gets angry and stings you on the arm.

MEANING

In life as you attempt to serve others, lead others, or influence others to do things that will help them grow, improve themselves, or

1

change their lives, you are attacked, criticized, or even "stung." What happens? What goes wrong, and why do others sometimes refuse your help? Why do they reject your leadership or refuse to be influenced by you? You have their best interest in mind. We know their refusal hurts them more than it hurts you. We say it is their fault, they should be smarter—but it is our fault.

How do you get others to want to do what you want them to do and be excited to do it? Let's find out and master the power of charisma, leadership, and influence.

THE POWER OF CHARISMA: KEY TO MAXIMUM SUCCESS

Have you ever noticed how some people can captivate, inspire, and influence others without effort? Other people instantly like them and want to be around them. Some individuals can enter a room and everyone notices. They seem always to get what they want because the people around them want to give it to them. How do they command such instant attention and influence everyone they meet?

This is the power of charisma. Charisma is a vital motivational and life skill that can and must be mastered if you are going to influence others. In this book, you will learn how you can harness this power of charisma.

I have spent my life studying persuasion, motivation, and influence. People often ask me what is the most important tool or skill in the entire influence toolbox? What is the one thing I can learn to achieve maximum success? The answer is simple. If there were one skill to master out of all the tools of persuasion and influence, it is charisma. It gives you the quickest return on your time and dramatically increases your success and income.

This vital success skill permeates every aspect of your life. Your career, your relationships, your ability to influence, and your income are all related to your ability to radiate charisma. Have you ever wondered why two people with the same education, the same contacts, the same IQ, and the same experience get dramatically different results from their lives? One enjoys massive success while the other one is barely making ends meet. Some call this simple luck, but when you have charisma you are guaranteed to have good luck. Imagine your success in life when you can automatically get others to willingly do what you want them to do, beg to do it, like to do it, and tell all their friends that they should also do it.

Charisma is the ability to empower and persuade others to believe in you, trust in you, and want to be influenced by you. You captivate and motivate them. You help them see themselves in the future carrying out your vision. They are moved and energized by your passion and enthusiasm. They are magnetized and driven by your charisma. They are lifted and inspired by your optimism and expectations. In essence, you're a source of empowerment, encouragement, and inspiration.

Mastering the various skills of charisma will propel you into a position of influence and success. People often wonder why achieving success is taking so long and why they have not learned even the basic skills to be successful or achieve their dreams. Charisma allows you to be more efficient and effective. Think about this. If others aren't responding to you or your attempts at influence, it probably is your fault. Sure, we like to say it is their fault, but when others are not influenced by you, empowered by you, or don't even want to help you—trust me—it is you.

I cannot stress enough that people of great influence have charisma. A study once asked participants to rate the top characteristic (out of 59 choices) of persuaders.[1] The number one characteristic was charisma. We can all think of charismatic people. They have a certain presence and charm about them; they are captivating and inspiring. They command our attention; we hang onto every word out of their mouths. Their presence prods us, motivates us, and inspires us. We feel better for having met them, seen them, and been influenced by them.

The challenge is that most of us think of charismatic people as movie stars, CEOs, politicians, or even religious leaders. These kinds of people might have a few of the tools of charisma and influence, but I want to reveal all the tools you can use in your efforts to influence and persuade. Some may call charisma magic, some call it luck, but when you master all these skills, you will achieve

---

1. R. G. Lord, R. J. Foti, and C. L. De Vader, "A Test of Leadership Categorization Theory: Internal Structure, Information Processing, and Leadership Perceptions," *Organizational Behavior and Human Performance*, Vol. 34 (1984), pp. 343–378.

more success. In fact, you'll wonder why success took so long and why it now seems so easy.

Charisma empowers others to like you, even if they don't know that much about you and even when there hasn't been enough time to develop trust in you. Charisma gives you power over, the allegiance of, and the devotion from your audience, and it creates instant support. So are you born with charisma or is it learned? Is it nature or nurture? The answer to both questions is yes! Some attributes are inherent, some you have learned, and others can be acquired. Charisma is a trait that can be taught and mastered, although it requires effort on your part. You may wonder—as I do— that if this skill is so important, if it is so valuable, if it is so critical to your success, why didn't they teach it to us in school? I can't answer that question, but I do have the answers you need to master the critical skill of charisma.

People today are less trusting, full of skepticism and more cynical than ever before. Corporate loyalty is a thing of the past. Belief in large business and government and society has eroded away. Everyone around us is confused, overwhelmed, and more difficult to influence than in the past. Now more than ever charisma is a vital and critical persuasion skill. The challenge is that some people think they have charisma, but they don't. Even if you can get somebody to do something, doesn't mean you are influential or charismatic. For example, if you are a manager, people do what you tell them to do because they feel they have to (even if they pretend to want to), but the results are only short term. If you are charismatic, however, people are devoted to you, want to work for you, and recruit everyone else to help you. In short, you have true influence over them.

DEFINING CHARISMA

When we hear the word "charisma," sometimes we are not sure what to think. What exactly is charisma? It can be a mysterious attribute. It's not assertiveness or enthusiasm, nor is it personality or being a so-called people person, although all of these traits seem to be a part of the package to one degree or another. You know when you have met or seen charismatic people. They are easy to spot and always radiate in a crowd of people. Sometimes identifying what makes someone charismatic is difficult, but you know when you feel and are moved by the power of charisma. When someone possesses the elusive quality of charisma, we feel honored and privileged to be associated with that person. Charisma is not just charm, devotion, likability, or passion. It is a feeling of confidence that does not overwhelm your audience but rather puts them at ease while maintaining credibility and rapport.

The word "charisma" comes from the Greek goddess Charis. Charis's character was one of total beauty and charity. How do others define charisma?

A rare, personal quality attributed to leaders who arouse fervent popular devotion and enthusiasm (*American Heritage Dictionary*)

Charisma is the ability to influence others positively by connecting with them physically, emotionally, and intellectually. (Dr. Tony Alessandra)[2]

Charisma is energy from the heart zone. If the speaker has no feeling, there is nothing to transfer. Charisma occurs when the speaker's feelings are transferred in the purest form to another. Charisma is not a diluted feeling. It is not disguised. It is a raw feeling. Charisma is the passing of our pure energy, our pure passion to the other. (Gerry Spence)[3]

Here's my own definition of charisma: the ability to easily build rapport, effectively influence others to your way of thinking, inspire them to achieve more, and in the process make an ally for life. In other words, charisma is being able to get others to want to do what you want them to do and be excited to do it. In fact, they are moved to get others onboard to also help your cause.

Is charisma good or bad? Is gravity good or bad? Just like gravity, charisma is neutral. It is how you use the power that defines you as good or bad. Some would say Adolf Hitler, Charles Manson, and Benito Mussolini had charisma, and they might have had a few

---

2. Tony Alessandra, *Charisma: Seven Keys to Developing the Magnetism That Leads to Success* (Business Plus, 2000).
3. Gerry Spence, *How to Argue and Win Every Time* (Pan Books, 1997).

of the tools of charisma. In many cases, people have had some of the skills of charisma and used them in an unethical way. You could probably count more people in history and in your life who had charisma and used it in a good and honorable way. So what is the difference?

Let's list the difference between the ethical and unethical uses of the power of charisma:

Ethical	*Unethical*
Serves others	Uses others
Creates win-win	Uses for selfish interests
Has high morals	Has low morals
Empowers people	Forces people
Opens up communication	Closes down communication
Follows the heart	Follows the money, power, or greed
Defines a vision and purpose	Makes it up along the way
Helps people grow	Bank account or ego grows
Works for the good of others	Works for own good
Helps society	Helps themselves

While I was doing research for this book, I conducted extensive interviews. I asked people how they would describe a person whom other people love to be around and want to be influenced by—whose presence captivates them and who makes them always want to achieve their potential. The word "charisma" came up the most to describe this skill. Is "charisma" the best word to describe the person who has instant influence over someone? I don't know, but I have not found a better word. If you have one please let me know.

HOW TO USE THIS BOOK

This book explores the power of charisma. Research on charisma shows that you must learn and master certain skills, traits, and attributes. I have determined that there are 30 in all, and each has a chapter of its own. The more of these tools you master, the more charismatic and influential you will become.

I recommend you read this book the first time from cover to cover. After you read about each trait or characteristic of charisma, rate yourself (be honest!) at the end of each chapter, and keep a tally of each score at the end of the book. Then reread the chapters a second time, working from your greatest weakness to your greatest strength. Read a chapter a day, and apply the technique and assignment found in the Charisma Key at the end of each chapter.

This book will help you master the art and science of charisma. Each chapter discusses one of the 30 critical skills or traits required to master charisma and includes:

- *Quote:* What has been said about this skill or trait?
- *Substance:* The core information needed to master the skill or trait.
- *Blind Spot:* The major blunder or mistake we usually make.
- *Application:* How you can apply and use the principle.
- *Example:* A current or historical example.
- *Charisma Key:* Something you can do and apply right away.

SELF-PERCEPTION BIAS: THE GREAT BLIND SPOT

What is the greatest roadblock to charisma? What is taking you so long to achieve true success or become a person of great influence? We all have blind spots in our lives that impede us from working on the things that can launch us into greater success. I call our inability to see these blind spots *self-perception bias*. We all tend to rate our skills and traits higher than they actually are. However, to improve, grow, and become more successful, we have to know our weaknesses and be able to identify our blind spots. If we don't know what they are, then we can never truly improve. We have to be honest with ourselves about our current levels of the skills, which I will show you how to identify in this book.

The reason self-perception bias has such a negative impact on our lives is because we tend to lie to ourselves. That's the bottom line. We are blind to the truth. We deceive ourselves. Denial is our happy place where we can cover up our weaknesses to protect our self-esteem. We set expectations that are not based on reality or honest evaluation. It might seem nice to view the world through rose-colored glasses for a while, but, in the end, we're setting ourselves up for failure. Self-perception bias manifests itself when we are evaluating a skill or talent that we expect ourselves to have or when others expect us to have that particular skill. When social pressure or social validation is involved, we make higher-than-expected evaluations of ourselves. Self-perception bias ultimately gives us an unrealistic view of reality and a false sense of security. We become numb to reality and fail to see exactly where we stand and what we need to improve.

We are good at judging others and pointing out what is wrong with them, but we don't seem to apply that same kind of analysis to ourselves. The same is true for our skills. We feel we must gloss over our weaknesses to make things seem better than they actually are. We have to have the ability to honestly access ourselves—both our strengths and weaknesses—and then find the necessary discipline to improve our faults.

To drive this point home, you need to discover your own weaknesses and be honest with your own personal reality. To enhance your success, your influence, and your charisma, you need to know exactly what skills you have mastered and which ones you need to work on. If you were in sales and you were asked to rate your ability to connect with people or your product knowledge, you would be 90 percent likely to rate yourself above average on these skills, even though mathematically the validity of your assertion should be around 50 percent.[4] You know all those poor managers you have met over the years? Over 90 percent of them will rate themselves better than the average manager. Did you know 80 percent of individuals perceive themselves as being brighter, better drivers, and more able entrepreneurs than their average peers?[5] One study even

---

4. Kurt W. Mortensen, *Persuasion IQ: The 10 Skills You Need to Get Exactly What You Want* (New York: AMACOM, 2008).

5. Isabelle Brocas and Juan D. Carrillo, "Are We All Better Drivers Than Average? Self-Perception and Biased Behaviour," CEPR Discussion Paper No. 3603 (October 2002).

found that most people believe themselves better than the average person in the following areas:[6]

- Athletics
- Intelligence
- Organization
- Ethic
- Logic
- Entertaining
- Fair-Minded[7]

THE SOLUTION

The solution is all about true self-assessment. When I teach influence or self-mastery seminars, I ask my students to list the top ten reasons for their lack of success. They find plenty of reasons why they are not at fault for their inability to achieve their goals, but they rarely take ownership of their weaknesses or admit that the fault could lie with them. You can always ask yourself:

- What are the skills and traits that I need to master to enhance my charisma?
- What do I keep trying to do and why do I keep failing?
- What are the missing skills that would turn my failures into success?
- What traits do I need to develop to take my life, my career, and my income to the next level?

All I am asking is for you to be open as you read the different categories of mastering charisma. Remember that we all have dif-

---

6. T. Gilovich, *How We Know What Isn't So: The Fallibility of Human Reason in Everyday Life* (New York: Free Press, 1991); S. E. Taylor and J. D. Brown, "Illusion and Well-being: A Social Psychological Perspective on Mental Health," *Psychological Bulletin*, 103 (1988), pp. 193–210.
7. D. G. Myers, *Social Psychology* (New York: McGraw Hill, 1987), pp. 444–445.

ferent strengths and weaknesses. Each chapter explains the common blind spots for each trait and a solution to implement easily. Try to honestly assess yourself or have someone you trust give you feedback. Charismatic people are able to take a good, hard look at themselves and come to grips with the facts, both the good and the bad. When you can do this, you are able to make real progress. If all else fails, go to www.lawsofcharisma.com to take your charisma assessment online (only if you can handle the nonsugar-coated truth).

ADDITIONAL CHARISMA RESOURCES AND AUDIOS (LAWSOFCHARISMA.COM)

- Support articles
- Section support audio: "Persuasion Resistance: The 10 Common Obstacles"
- Section worksheet

PRESENCE:
WHAT DO YOU RADIATE?

FABLE: THE TURKEY AND THE PEACOCKS

One day, a turkey left his pack of friends and ventured into a large meadow where peacocks were known to live. He looked around and did not see any of the peacocks. As he roamed and explored, searching for the peacocks, he found a few piles of beautiful feathers. The turkey decided that he wanted the prestige of a peacock. He took the fallen peacock feathers, tied them to his tail feathers, and paraded around the meadow. When he saw the peacocks returning, he strutted toward them to see whether they could tell that he was a turkey. As he neared the peacocks, they discovered his bluff and began to peck at this head and pluck away his false feathers. The turkey ran back to the other turkeys, who had been watching from a distance. They, however, were even more upset with his display and began to chase him around and peck at his head.

Meaning: When you fake your presence, you falsify who you are. When you fake your passion or fake your confidence, no one is fooled. People will always judge you by your appearance, presence, and demeanor. Are you trying to be something or someone you are not? People can sense a fake presence. True congruent presence is power. Your presence is the key to developing instant charisma.

COMMANDING PRESENCE SKILLS/TRAITS

- Passion
- Confidence
- Congruence
- Optimism
- Positive power
- Energy and balance
- Humor and happiness

CHAPTER 1

PASSION:
THE TRANSFER OF PURE ENERGY

One person with passion is better than forty people merely
interested.
—E. M. FORSTER

People who know where they are going are able to captivate others
because they are passionate and therefore charismatic. You can tell
when you meet them or when they enter a room. Others are drawn
to them because, deep down, people want to be passionate about
something. When others see that passion in your eyes, you become
more charismatic. They sense that you can help them and improve
their lives. This does not guarantee that everyone will like you, but
others will respect you for your conviction and your passion.

Passion is critical to influencing others and transmitting charisma. Charismatic people radiate heartfelt passion. When your audience can sense your passion and sincere conviction for your

cause, they will jump on board emotionally. We all love people who are excited and filled with believable passion for their subject. When you have passion for something, you want to let everyone know about it. You want to convert as many people to your cause as possible. Even when someone disagrees with you, you are able to openly listen to their opinions, feedback, and point of view while maintaining your composure and conviction.

Passion is very contagious. When you transfer your passion, the people around you start to absorb your energy. They begin to perform better. Being on the job no longer seems like work. They become more proactive, more willing to work as a team, and more optimistic. When you have tapped into your passion, you become more determined, and that determination strengthens your persistence.

A word of caution: Even when you are passionate, do not forego learning the skills you need to be successful. Passion is a critical piece of the charisma pie, but you still need the other pieces of the pie to radiate powerful long-term charisma.

Passion always includes enthusiasm, but you can be enthusiastic without having passion. Enthusiasm is a strong excitement or feeling on behalf of a cause. You have probably seen charismatic people who give off enthusiasm. It is in their faces and their demeanor—they are undeniably motivated—and it creates sparks of curiosity. Enthusiasm not only reduces worry and fear, but it also creates confidence, compassion, and a synchronization between you and your audience.

BLIND SPOT

Most people have trouble tapping into their true passion. Many confuse hype, extra caffeine, or excitement with passion. Passion is not running around and bouncing up and down like a new puppy. True passion radiates and captivates and does not need to be forced. When your audience feels forced or unrealistic hype on your part, they will be repelled. You will be seen as fake, and that perception will decrease your ability to influence. Tap into your true passion, and it will influence others to come around to your point of view. Just because you are excited does not mean you radiate passion. Make sure you are radiating true passion, not false enthusiasm or hype.

APPLICATION

Those with charisma increase enthusiasm by gaining insight and knowledge about their subject. They have developed a true belief and conviction in what they do. Believe in yourself and in your message, radiate enthusiasm in all that you do. On the flip side, fake enthusiasm, unrealistic hype, and false energy destroy charisma. You can enhance your charisma by doing the following:

- Always maintain your credibility.
- Be sincere in all your interactions.
- Always be connecting with others.
- Always be authentic.
- Maintain constant confidence.

EXAMPLE

John Wooden is a great example of passion. Everyone around him, especially his players, felt his passion and was influenced by it. He was UCLA's basketball coach during the team's greatest era. He recruited raw talent, demanded they practice hard, and provided passion, enthusiasm, and inspiration. His teams won 665 games in 27 seasons and 10 NCAA titles during his last 12 seasons. His teams hold the all-time record of winning 88 games in a row and had an incredible four perfect seasons. He never made more than $35,000 a year, but his passion and impact on the fans and on his players will last a lifetime. He loved what he was doing and proved that passion is a critical element of success.

CHARISMA KEY

Find your passion. Tapping into your passion is like sculpting. You are getting a little closer each time you take a chip off the raw stone.

Sometimes we get closer to our passion by finding things we don't want to do. Start experimenting with different tasks and topics, and get to know other people. You don't know whether you like a certain food unless you are willing to take a bite. Read more, join more clubs, and spend more time on personal development in the areas that might be worthy of your passion. You cannot be passionate about something if you don't know anything about it. In fact, educating yourself about a topic is a great way to increase your passion.

Here is the question I want you to think about today: When it comes to what you are doing with your life, are you singing the song and really feeling it, or are you just singing the words—going through the motions? Think about your answer.

Rate Your Passion
Add your score to page 182.

0	1	2	3	4	5	6	7	8	9	10
Poor		*Weak*			*Average*		*Strong*			*Perfect*

CHAPTER 2

CONFIDENCE:
CONVICTION IS CONTAGIOUS

Without a humble but reasonable confidence in your own
powers you cannot be successful or happy.
— Norman Vincent Peale

Confidence is a trait that increases your charisma and attracts people to you. People love to follow and be influenced by others who
are confident in themselves and their abilities. Most people you
meet suffer in the self-confidence arena, but your high confidence
will make up for their shortfall. Confidence breeds trust. Demonstrating confidence in your field, in your industry, and in your life
increases the confidence of others in you. The people we admire
and look up to the most are usually the type of people who know
what they want and have the confidence to get it.

You must learn to communicate with great confidence and authority. The perception of confidence is critical to maintaining cha-

risma. The higher your true confidence is, the more charisma you radiate. People read your confidence in your tone of voice, body language, and other subconscious triggers.

True confidence is a state of mind. At times in your life and in your career, your personal confidence can get smashed and needs to be rebuilt. Charismatic people can maintain confidence in all situations even if they have encountered defeats, setbacks, or unpredicted outcomes. We all have a tendency to feel insufficient or inferior at times. When you lose faith in yourself or have had failures in your life, you lose confidence through fear, which can be defined simply as magnified doubt. All worries, questions, concerns, and insecurities can ultimately be traced back to fear in one form or another.

Fear breeds doubt and doubt destroys confidence. You need to make sure that your confidence is bigger than your doubts. What does your audience really sense in you? Are you afraid to exercise confidence and charisma? The desire to overcome your fear needs to be bigger than the fear itself. While it is okay to have fear, you must be able to handle and manage that fear. When you doubt yourself and your abilities, others will doubt you and your charisma.

Other factors that can destroy confidence are:

● Negative thoughts.
● Indecision about purpose.
● Worry.

People who lack confidence will always struggle to effectively influence others and create charisma. Even when you have confidence, you can still sometimes feel fear, tension, or uneasiness. Confidence is the ability to control these feelings. If you're perceived as underconfident, your audience will feel that way too—about your product, about you, or about your idea. Don't panic if you don't feel confident at every encounter; confidence will come with time. Complete confidence takes experience, practice, and patience.

You may be wondering, "Can't overconfidence hurt my ability to exude charisma?" Of course! You must not come across as condescending or arrogant. How can you tell the difference between confidence and cockiness? It's all about your intention. Confidence is motivated by a sincere desire to help others and to make a difference. True confidence comes from knowing that you have the tools, resources, and ability to do the job that's expected of you. In contrast, cockiness is driven by a need to help yourself, instead of helping others. Deep down, cockiness actually reveals insecurity—the very opposite of confidence.

Arrogant individuals seek approval and recognition for all the wrong reasons and in all the wrong ways. Arrogance makes someone self-centered, whereas confidence makes a person people-centered. Arrogance is about self and confidence is about others. Whether you say and do all the right things simply doesn't matter. If you lack confidence, the cause is lost. Even if people like you, the lack of confidence destroys your ability to influence and have charisma.

BLIND SPOT

How you think you are coming across and how you are actually perceived are usually two completely different things. How do others really perceive you? Are you focused on them or on yourself? You think you have confidence, you feel confident, and you think you come across as confident, but you could be perceived as either arrogant, cocky, or condescending. There is a fine line between being confident and coming across as arrogant. That is the blind spot. The flip side is the lack of confidence that could trigger fear and lack of trust in those you attempt to influence. Bottom line: no confidence, no charisma.

APPLICATION

Here are some additional ways you can avoid the trap of seeming overly confident or arrogant:

- Always take feedback or criticism with an open heart.
- Spend more time listening than talking.
- Be able to admit that you were wrong.

- Don't always attempt to prove you are right.

- Ask questions to demonstrate concern.

- Have someone else explain why you are credible.

EXAMPLE

In the sports world, the name of Joe Namath comes up when you hear the word confidence. He played for the New York Jets when they were part of the American Football League (AFL). They made it to the Super Bowl III to play the powerful Baltimore Colts, at a time when no one thought an AFL team could compete with a National Football League (NFL) team. The previous two Super Bowls were complete blowouts for the NFL over the AFL. The Jets were 17-point underdogs. Joe Namath was being heckled at a press conference, and then, with great confidence and authority, he said, "I guarantee we will beat the Baltimore Colts." His confidence rallied his team to win that Super Bowl, 16–7, and Joe Namath won the MVP title. The rest is history.

CHARISMA KEY

One thing that can hurt your perception of confidence is embarrassment—from being worried about what others will think of you, about failing publicly, or about breaking a social rule. The best way to handle embarrassment is to understand that most people are sympathetic if you handle your embarrassment the right way. The studies show that those who acknowledge their embarrassment are more liked than those who deny it. You are human and embarrassment is a human emotion. Admit it, smile or laugh about it, and move on. No one does everything right, and your audience will understand if you acknowledge your mistake or your embarrassment. Even when you help someone become less embarrassed, your likeability goes up. When you build your confidence, the chance of your being embarrassed goes down dramatically.

Today, either acknowledge your embarrassment or help some-one feel less embarrassed.

Rate Your Confidence
Add your score to page 182.

0	1	2	3	4	5	6	7	8	9	10
Poor		*Weak*			*Average*		*Strong*			*Perfect*

CHAPTER 3

CONGRUENCE:
ACTION VERSUS INTENTION

You can fool some of the people all of the time, and all of the
people some of the time, but you cannot fool all of the people
all the time.

—ABRAHAM LINCOLN

Agreement and harmony between what you say and what you do
are paramount to instilling trust and generating charisma. The more
consistent and congruent you are in every aspect of your message,
the more honest and genuine you'll be perceived to be. If you don't
believe in your message, others won't believe in it. When you practice
what you preach, they will start to practice what you preach. When
you achieve congruency, you will become more authentic. This au-
thenticity is what helps you magnify your charisma and draws people to you. When you possess congruency, you don't need to
manipulate, hide, or camouflage your behavior or your message.

Congruence opens the door to influence and charisma. It increases your believability and likeability. You attain congruency when your message is synchronized with your beliefs and values. It occurs when your voice, body language, words, and vocal tone are all congruent and aligned. It comes from making sure your verbal and nonverbal messages are in agreement. Congruence is even more important when your topic is highly emotional. To enhance your charisma, your complete message has to be congruent. When your messages are not in agreement, you come across as not so trustworthy, doubtful, less than knowledgeable. and lacking in charisma.

Think about your overall history and, more specifically, your last interaction. Were you congruent? Does your nonverbal behavior match your actions? Are you sure? Are your emotions congruent with your message? When your past encounters don't align with your message, the mismatch triggers incongruence. The feelings of incongruence will usually manifest as a gut feeling. Suspicion will increase, and your audience will start to look for things that are wrong with you or your message. Distrust causes your charisma to plunge. Your inconsistency will decrease your ability to gain influence because humans can be natural lie detectors. When we attempt to fake congruence, we spend most of our time and mental energy trying to fake our message, triggering incongruence.

Deception, of course, is wrong—no doubt about it. But you can trigger incongruence simply because you get nervous or uneasy and inadvertently show signs of deception. Sometimes, even if you are telling the truth and think you are congruent, you might be sending subliminal signals of incongruency and deception. The audience can't always identify exactly what is making them distrustful, but they feel that way and that is all that matters. We all show micro expressions that happen so rapidly that the conscious mind can't perceive them, but the subconscious can sense them. Micro expressions are quick facial mannerisms that reveal deception or nervousness.

Another thing that causes a blip on your audience's deception radar is a disconnect between your emotion and your reaction. For example, if you make an angry face, then pound the table with your hand five seconds later, obviously you are not feeling that emotion. Be careful that you are congruent with every aspect of your message.

Congruence is simple to understand and difficult for many people to achieve. You waste mental energy when you are trying to remember a past lie or what you said in the last encounter. Attempts to deceive just suck the energy and life out of you and your presentation, causing your audience to sense that something is wrong. When you tell the truth, are consistent, and know what you believe, you are naturally congruent and more charismatic.

BLIND SPOT

Even when you feel congruent, you may not look congruent. Whether you are deceiving or not, whether you are insincere or not, you might be coming across as if you are. A little fib? A white lie? No one will know. We think others can't tell. They haven't said anything about not believing you or your message. A little deception has worked before, and no one has called you on it. Most people can sense incongruence and rarely will say anything about it. Every gesture and movement you make will either attract or repel your audience. You will either come across as congruent or incongruent. People are reading you like a book. Do your gestures match your message?

APPLICATION

Everyone can pick up on your nonverbal behavior. We sense something is not quite right. Others will sense any form of incongruence or deception radiating from you. Be aware that many of your current nonverbal actions will trigger incongruence. They might be a natural part of your behavior, but they could look like deception. Here some things that can trigger a sense of deception:

- Forced eye contact
- Shifting back in chair
- Rubbing or touching lips
- Scratching your face
- Dilated pupils

- Yawning
- Rising voice pitch

EXAMPLE

Mahatma Gandhi is a great example of someone who was congruent. He spent many years in prison and led many nonviolent campaigns for civil rights and against taxation, poverty, and discrimination. His biggest victory was the independence of India from a foreign power. Everyone knew that what he said, what he did, and how he felt were all the same. Once he was invited to speak in England to the House of Commons. He spoke and captivated the audience for over two hours with no notes and no preparation. Even after a speech of that length, he got a standing ovation from a very skeptical audience. They asked his personal assistant how he could speak so long without any notes. The assistant said, "Gandhi says what he feels and says what he thinks; they are one in the same."

CHARISMA KEY

Watch your gestures, your body language, and your vocal tones. Are they congruent? The best (and most painful) way to reduce the degree of incongruence in your messages is to record a video of yourself. When you watch yourself, you can pick up things you never knew you were doing that detract from or destroy your message. When you really get brave, you can have a colleague watch the video with you for some genuine feedback. Just remember that every gesture, word, or tone of voice will either say "congruent" or "incongruent." Don't delay doing this; do it today.

Rate Your Congruence
Add your score to page 182.

0	1	2	3	4	5	6	7	8	9	10
Poor		*Weak*			*Average*		*Strong*			*Perfect*

CHAPTER 4

OPTIMISM:
ADJUST ATTITUDES

A pessimist sees the difficulty in every opportunity; an
optimist sees the opportunity in every difficulty.
— WINSTON CHURCHILL

The majority of wealthy and successful business executives attribute their success to their optimism and attitude more than any other factor. How can you inspire people and transfer charisma if you don't have the right attitude or an optimistic outlook? Your attitude about the rain on your Hawaiian vacation can either ruin your vacation or make it more fun and more memorable. Optimism tells you that your problems are only temporary, and pessimism tells you they are permanent and there's no way out. As an optimist, you will attract people to your cause and radiate charisma. Studies have shown that optimists do better in school, perform better in their careers, and live longer than pessimists. Pessimists tend to battle depression and give up more easily.

Optimism is more than PMA (positive mental attitude). It is more than constantly saying positive things to others and hoping they will come true. True optimism is a frame of mind that governs how you look at the world. Optimism means having expectations that things will eventually turn out okay. Being optimistic means that you firmly believe that you will eventually accomplish everything you set out to do and that you will be able to help others achieve their goals. When you are truly optimistic, you can transfer your hope and courage to others.

Optimism means that you tend to see mostly the positive in all situations. Rather than focusing on the negative, you always look for ways to move forward. People will gravitate to those who have a positive view on life. As an optimist, you see the world as a series of exciting challenges that you can conquer. You inspire positive feelings, which are contagious. You will empower people to believe in themselves and in their future. When you are optimistic, you help others see failure or setbacks as temporary. Optimists know that, when failure happens, they have something to learn in their lives or something they need to adjust. A pessimist, on the other hand, calls failure a permanent weakness and/or blames someone else. Optimism, then, is the ability to bounce back sooner rather than later.

Attitude is a subset of optimism, a reflection of what is happening inside a person. Most people don't spend time thinking about their attitudes, yet they allow their attitudes to control them throughout the day. Attitude is a habit that arises from our expectations: what we expect of ourselves and of others. You can influence others with the right attitude. When we master influence, we know that our attitude, our optimism, and our expectations are critical in getting others to take action. Your charisma, your attitude, and your expectations will be reflected by the person you are attempting to influence.

No one can influence others in the long term with a negative attitude. You become charismatic when you are able to turn other people's negativity into something more positive. You must learn to look at the world in a different way. You must move away from drowning yourself in the current challenge and spend time looking for the solution. When you hit bumps in the road, you don't stop, whine, complain, or think it's not fair. You look for other resources, strategies to make it past the bumps. An optimistic attitude allows you to takes risks, but you always know things will work out. It increases your resilience when faced with challenges, and you automatically become more creative, motivated, and flexible. Optimism allows you to exude charisma.

BLIND SPOT

We are born pretty optimistic. Life beats us up, things happen to us, and naturally we become more and more pessimistic. Then pessimism increases over time. When this happens, we attract pessimistic people into our lives, and we usually don't even realize or notice this subtle change. We still think we're optimistic, but we actually have turned to the dark side and don't even know it. Take a realistic look at how you look at life. Are you really an optimist, or has pessimism crept into your life? Do you really feel things will work out and expect the most of yourself and others? The bottom line is that you can become more optimistic. Pessimism repels charisma.

APPLICATION

You can improve your optimism in specific ways. Use the following methods to improve your optimism and, in turn, your ability to influence others and have charisma.

- Choose to be optimistic.
- Take responsibility for your life and never blame others.
- Build on current success and past victories.
- Associate with positive people.
- Watch the way you talk to yourself. Keep it positive.
- Stay healthy and always exercise.
- Create the ability to quickly turn a negative mood into a positive one.

EXAMPLE

Lance Armstrong is my favorite example of optimism. Lance won two Tour de France stages before the age of 25. After that he was diagnosed with testicular cancer, which spread to his lungs, abdomen, and brain. He had surgery, and his doctors gave him only a 50 percent chance of living. His optimism, attitude, and expectation of living are not only why he is alive, but also the reason he went on to win seven consecutive Tour de Frances, as well as becoming athlete of the year in 1999. He is the only person who has won that many races. Many could have viewed the cancer diagnosis as a complete setback, a no-win situation, but Lance's optimism saw it as only a bump in the road.

CHARISMA KEY

Do you ever feel that pessimism's grip is around your throat? You feel you want to be the opposite, but you are naturally programmed to be pessimistic. If everyone around you pulls you down with their pessimism, there is a solution. Try to see the potential positive outcomes of all the challenges you are facing. Don't be so sensitive to the criticism of others or so concerned about what others think of you. Quit looking for possible signs of setback or failure. Today, try to look for what is turning out right instead of what is going wrong. Control your relationships and spend more time with optimistic people. Find others who are willing to help you past the bumps in the road. When you are feeling down—when you are feeling low—take the time to give back and serve someone. It will do wonders for your optimism and your attitude.

Rate Your Optimism
Add your score to page 182.

0	1	2	3	4	5	6	7	8	9	10
Poor		*Weak*			*Average*		*Strong*		*Perfect*	

CHAPTER 5

POSITIVE POWER:
FORCE IS NOT CHARISMA

I would rather try to persuade a man to go along, because once
I have persuaded him he will stick. If I scare him, he will stay
just as long as he is scared, and then he is gone.

—GENERAL DWIGHT DAVID EISENHOWER

Power comes in many forms. Certain forms of power increase our
perceived charisma and our ability to influence. When we have legitimate forms of power, people will be more willing and want to
take action. When used in the wrong way, power will backfire on
you in the long term.

Nearly every organization has some type of authority structure.
Rules (written and unwritten) dictate how people are to react to
power and authority. Managers always think they have great
power, but usually they have much less than they think. The ability
to reward and punish is not the power that will help in your ability

to radiate charisma. Your internal power will always outlast external power.

Charismatic people instinctively know and understand how to use different forms of positive power. Power builds when you can help others get something they need or want. Power is different from force. Power creates trust, it strengthens, and it enables. Force must always be maintained, enforced, and warranted. Force sucks the energy and life out of people. True power encourages and creates unity and synergy. Power causes us to listen and obey. Force causes us to be skeptical and run. Charismatic people don't have power trips or feel the need to force themselves on others or make others do things just for fun. They understand how to use the proper forms of power for their ethical purpose. Positive power opens up their audiences and enhances their charisma. Knowledge, expertise, and authority are all forms of positive power.

A form of power that helps you develop charisma is understanding authority power, which is based on how other people perceive your knowledge level, position, or expertise. You have this power when others believe you have specific knowledge they need or hold a higher position than they do. This type of authority enables those in a power position to influence others to comply because of their status, position, or rank. CEOs of large corporations and police officers wield this form of power. You feel compelled to comply with the head boss or the police based on their positions of authority.

Exercising authority power does not mean being egotistical or condescending. Your audience has certain expectations that you can help and advise them in solving their problem. The help could take the form of a product or a service, rewards, or a contact. People want to be led in the right direction by a competent and knowledgeable person. If that competent and knowledgeable person is you, then you have power and charisma. Think of yourself as a consultant or advisor. You're not selling anything; you're helping them make the right decision. Looking at charisma or influence in this manner changes everyone's perspective. You become the authority figure, and everyone is programmed to follow the authority they trust. When you can prove that you are an expert, skilled, or capable, you gain authority power.

Another form of power comes from how we dress. You can create instant impressions of power with what you wear, such as a uniform. Your uniform could be a business suit, a military uniform, or any type of identifying clothing. Your uniform or clothes can evoke authority or even instant prestige. When you wear the right clothes or uniform for the situation, you can influence and build charisma before you speak.

The last form of perceived power is known as title power. For example, the titles "president," "CEO," "esquire," "manager," or "captain" create certain expectations of authority and respect. For example, when we hear "doctor" in front of a name, we automatically expect the person to be important and/or intelligent. We don't even ask whether he or she graduated at the top of the class or even whether he or she is any good as a doctor. When you hold a title that projects respect and attention, your ability to influence is strengthened. Find a title that is appropriate for you and your work. For example, "vice president," "senior partner," "managing director," or "account executive" might work to increase your power.

BLIND SPOT

The blind spot is not understanding that power itself is neutral and that we can use power in good ways or bad. For some reason, talking about power makes us a little nervous. The challenge is that most of our experience with power has been negative. A certain kind of boss may say, "Do it or you are fired." Sure, it tends to work for the short term, but it is not a good form of power or influence. Fear has a time and place, but it diminishes your ability to radiate long-term charisma. Getting past the blind spot takes realizing that power can be a very good thing. People naturally want to follow good forms of power. Power helps radiate your charisma. Most people are blind to the fact that they have some of the forms of good power but don't know it or how to use it.

APPLICATION

Even if you have legitimate forms of power, you are probably doing things that will drain your power. Here are some:

- *Overload of Seriousness:* We all need to lighten up every once in awhile.

- *Appearance:* The way you dress for the occasion can detract from your authority.

- *Poor Presentation Skills:* Rambling or using vocal fillers is not effective.

- *Power Going to Your Head:* Even if you don't do so intentionally, you can come across as if you are master of the universe.

- *Serving Yourself Instead of Others:* Ego gets in the way of positive power.

- *Not Showing Respect to Others:* This includes the competition.

EXAMPLE

Consider the power of the Dalai Lama, the title belonging to a line of Tibetan religious leaders. He is the spiritual leader of Tibet. The Dalai Lama is believed to be reborn in order to be able to enlighten others. The current Dalai Lama (the 14th) won the Nobel Peace Prize in 1989. This position is an excellent example of power. The Dalai Lama has the power to influence his followers, but he has no power over nonfollowers. Power can be very situational and vary from person to person. If you were a follower of the Dalai Lama and met him, you would feel his instant power over you, which comes from his position and title. He could have personal power over you before you even exchange a word.

CHARISMA KEY

Do you have the real authority to lead and guide others with charisma? The key is to choose one form of power and enhance it. Get started now. Expertise is the easiest form of power to implement. Do you know your product, competition, forecasts, or industry? Do you have the specific knowledge your audience is looking for?

Being able to solve your audience's problem makes it much easier to influence them. When you have legitimate power, people put up no resistance and want you to influence them.

Enhancing your title is another form of power that can be easily implemented. Today, create a title for yourself that will enhance your perceived power. Make sure it is a title that automatically garners respect. Of course, make sure it is one you can appropriately adopt.

Rate Your Positive Power
Add your score to page 182.

0	1	2	3	4	5	6	7	8	9	10
Poor		*Weak*			*Average*		*Strong*		*Perfect*	

CHAPTER 6

ENERGY AND BALANCE:
VIBRANT WELL-BEING

The higher your energy level, the more efficient your body.
The more efficient your body, the better you feel and the more
you will use your talent to produce outstanding results.
—ANTHONY ROBBINS

You have seen it, you have felt it. When you are around a charismatic person, not only do you feel their energy, but it is transferred to you. Too many people project such low energy that they can actually repel those they are trying to influence. You probably have sat next to someone like this. You don't even talk to them, but you can feel them draining the energy out of you.

You need to find the time and the will to create your own personal health plan. People judge you by how you look and how you make them feel. You need to consider your weight, your exercise, your nutrition, and your sleep. We're all busy, and I know making time for these things is difficult, but it is critical for your success and your ability to influence and radiate charisma.

When you enter a room, everyone needs to notice you. When you have energy and charisma, you are transferring energy. When you are speaking in front of a group, you not only have to transmit energy to the audience, but increase the energy in the room throughout your presentation. A bored and uninterested mind will always say no. When your presentation or demeanor is dull and lifeless, you lose their interest and transmit no charisma.

When we look at life, we have to realize that it is not lived in segments, but rather, it is part of a greater whole. We can't compartmentalize each area of our lives. Every aspect of your life will either help or hurt your charisma. Your objective is to get all areas working together to create and transfer high energy. Realize, however, that you can invest too much time in one aspect of your life. When you do, you can get unbalanced. Even too much of a good thing can lead to disaster.

Charismatic and successful people enhance their energy by finding balance and alignment in their lives. No balance plus no energy equals no charisma. When you don't feel right, you don't seem right to other people. Make sure you maintain a balance in every aspect of your life. Imbalance can destroy motivation, and decrease your energy. Most people lack energy because they don't know that an imbalance exists. Maybe only one area of your life is out of alignment, but it can still have a direct effect on other areas of our life. A good analogy is your car. If the brakes aren't working, it will affect your ability to drive. Find balance and you will find more energy.

If you want balance, if you want more focus and energy, you need to align your life. There are six areas that you must spend time on each week (some require more time than others). These are the six areas of life alignment—

1. *Financial:* If you can't take care of your monetary needs, you can't take care of your basic needs. If you neglect your finances, imbalance will ensue. We all know that, when you can't pay the bills, it affects every aspect of your life.
2. *Physical:* If you don't feel well, you can't even begin to think about improving the other aspects of your life. You need to

have a good health plan. Do you understand the importance of nutrition, sleep, and exercise? If you don't, your lack of health and energy will decrease your ability to find balance and generate charisma.

3. *Emotional:* As human beings, we are emotional creatures. You cannot allow emotions like anger, resentment, frustration, hate, and depression rule your life. You're in control. If you can't control your emotions, you will be unable to control your actions or your life. Emotional mastery is essential to a balanced, happy personal life.

4. *Intellectual:* Personal development keeps you excited, motivated, and moving toward our goals. We are at our best when we are continually learning and improving. We need to do personal betterment every day because a lack of it causes us to become negative, cynical, and pessimistic.

5. *Spiritual:* You have to be in tune with yourself, with who you are, and with your purpose. We are spiritual beings; we all have a spiritual side. We each define spirituality in a different way: serving others, practicing a religion, meditating, or even getting back to nature. You need to take the time to listen to your inner voice and to tap into your personal spirituality.

6. *Social:* We are also social creatures. Our greatest strength and well-being come from our relationships. Most of our happiness and sadness come from our associations with each other. As such, relationships are an integral part of your happiness and balance. You need a sense of meaning and purpose to lead a fulfilled life. No man is an island, and life and success are not solo projects.

We always need to make sure that we are growing and that we are continually investing in the right areas of our life. We often spend too much of our time focusing on the wrong things, those that have no value or are of no use to us. We get so busy pursuing what others recommend that we forget to examine what is helping or hurting our balance and energy. If we neglect any one of the life-alignment areas, our overall happiness, energy, and success will diminish.

BLIND SPOT

I have said it, you have said it: "I don't have time to exercise." If you want charisma and if you want to radiate energy, you have to possess the inner health required to radiate energy. This blind spot entails a failure to see that nutrition, relationships, exercise, and especially having a balance in life give us more energy and more time. When we exercise, we sleep less, think better, accomplish more in less time, and live longer. The blunt truth is that every minute we spend on our health, energy, and nutrition is returned to us tenfold. It is worth your time; so make the time.

APPLICATION

If you are giving a presentation to a group, energy in the room is everything. No energy means no influence and no charisma. Here are some things you can do during a presentation that can increase the energy and involvement in the room.

- Have the audience stand up, move around, or raise their hands.
- Do a group exercise that generates movement or interactivity.
- Ask a thought-provoking question.
- Tell a powerful story.
- Get them to laugh.

EXAMPLE

When I think of energy and charisma, I think of Anthony Robbins. He started his career promoting seminars for Jim Rohn and later started to teach aspects of neurolinguistic programming. He is the author of *Unlimited Power* and famous for having everyone in his audience walk on fire. You probably have seen him on infomercials promoting personal development programs. Watch him and you will see the definition of energy and charisma. He can engage an audience for four straight days, and those events last very late into the evening. He is so powerful, engaging, and full of energy that his audience doesn't realize they have been with Tony for over 12 hours. His transfer of energy causes him to be charismatic.

CHARISMA KEY

The key in this section is to discover what is sucking the energy out of you. What is happening during the day that causes your energy to fall? The lack of balance in your life could be a major factor in your losing valuable energy. Find the biggest area of weakness (physical, intellectual, spiritual, social, financial, or emotional), and create a game plan to fix it. Try to find your weakest link and come up with a game plan to improve that area. Fear of failure, lack of confidence, or criticism will also lower your energy output. Having no passion, no balance, or a negative attitude can also decrease your energy.

Rate Your Energy and Balance
Add your score to page 182.

0	1	2	3	4	5	6	7	8	9	10
Poor		*Weak*			*Average*		*Strong*			*Perfect*

CHAPTER 7

HUMOR AND HAPPINESS:
IT COMES FROM WITHIN

Happiness cannot come from without. It must come from
within. It is not what we see and touch or that which others do
for us which makes us happy; it is that which we think and feel
and do, first for the other fellow and then for ourselves.

—HELEN KELLER

When you have true charisma, you are happy and you radiate happiness. So many people are searching for this happiness that, when
they feel it in you, they gravitate toward you. This means you love
and enjoy life and others love to be around you. You attract people
to you. Others may define happiness in terms of fame, fortune, success, or wealth, but notice that every single one of these is external.
What is happening inside a person is the biggest gauge of happi-

ness. We think we will be happy when we finally make our fortune, graduate from college, retire, are promoted, or end up at the top of our business. But lasting happiness is rooted in the now, not the future.

Most unhappiness is simply your own interpretation of things that are happening in your life: your mental state, emotional baggage, or physical well-being. Recall a time when you were truly happy. What were you doing? What things were going through your mind? You probably felt an inner peace and security about what you were doing and the direction you were headed. Happiness usually includes the steady advancement toward an exciting goal or objective—being headed in a direction that is part of your purpose and passion. Regardless of the external factors in your life, you will feel happiness when you feel a sense of purpose and direction. You are able to transmit this to your audience and thereby increase their happiness.

The use of humor and your ability to transmit charisma are directly correlated. Humor disarms people and opens them up, making them more likely to connect with you and feel your charisma. We are drawn to people who make us smile and help us feel better about ourselves or external circumstances. This brand of humor enables audiences to be more receptive. Also, they will remember you and continue to hold you in a positive light even after the initial encounter. When you leverage humor, your message receives more weight and consideration than one that comes from someone who has not created the audience rapport or charisma you have obtained.

The benefits of humor are countless and critical for your charisma. You don't have to be a stand-up comedian, but you can get someone to smile or even laugh. This humor keeps people's minds from wandering during your encounter and reenergizes their souls. In short, it puts them in a good mood and eases their daily tensions. So what does it do for you? The proper use of humor will boost your confidence and increase your likability. It enables you to establish instant rapport so that people will trust you more. Practice your humor. Make sure it works. You want others to laugh with you, not feel sorry for you.

BLIND SPOT

Oh, how blind we can be! There are no reset buttons or do-overs in life. This is our life and we need to enjoy the journey. Thinking that we will be happy when [*fill in the blank*] destroys our ability to enjoy the now and to radiate contentment and charisma. Expecting the external things of life to bring us happiness is a slippery slope. They might bring temporary happiness, but our goal should be long-term happiness. We are blind because most of the things we are pursuing don't bring true long-term happiness.

APPLICATION

Don't worry if the people in the audience don't laugh or even crack a smile. Some people won't laugh or smile at anything. They might be smiling on the inside, or they may just want to stay miserable. Focus on the people you can touch or help to smile and laugh. Learn to laugh at yourself. Self-deprecating humor is a great way to connect with your audience. They know that you make mistakes just like them, and your mistakes make them more comfortable to be around you. Always be prepared to have fun, always try to share your happiness, and always be ready to use your sense of humor. When you can use your sense of humor, you are able to help others:

- Become more open with their feelings.
- Reduce their stress and fear.
- Experience more life satisfaction.
- Enhance their self-image.
- Become friendlier.

EXAMPLE

A great example of contentment is Victor Frankl, a psychiatrist who survived the terror and brutality of the Nazi concentration camps. He stated in his well-known book *Man's Search for Meaning*: "Happiness is a condition rather than a destination. Happiness cannot be pursued. The more we aim at happiness, the more we miss our aim. If there is a reason for happiness, happiness ensues. It is a side effect of having a purpose and meaning to life." Frankl had every reason to embrace unhappiness. In 1942 he was imprisoned by the Nazis, along with his wife and his parents. In the concentration camp, he worked as a general practitioner, encountering and witnessing countless instances of suffering and brutality. Even through all the horrors he experienced, he concluded that people can find happiness and meaning in any situation.

CHARISMA KEY

What can you do today to increase your happiness and enhance your charisma? Are you really happy? Our quality of life is the best it has ever been, but happiness tends to be at an all-time low. Why?

- First, we feel tension, which creates unhappiness because of the many conflicting goals in our lives. We have goals and aspirations in life that conflict with one other (e.g., become an entrepreneur or have a secure job), thereby causing incredible stress and personal tension. Take the time today to figure out what goals conflict in your life, find a solution, and see increased happiness.
- Second, we have no meaningful goals. Discover a fun, exciting, realistic goal and pursue it, and you will find an instant step-up in your happiness.

Rate Your Humor and Happiness
Add your score to page 182.

0	1	2	3	4	5	6	7	8	9	10
Poor		*Weak*			*Average*		*Strong*		*Perfect*	

PRESENCE RESOURCES (LAWSOFCHARISMA.COM)

- Support articles
- Section support audio: "Establishing Automatic Trust"
- Section worksheet

CORE QUALITIES:
THE INSIDE DICTATES THE OUTSIDE

FABLE: THE WOOD-CHOPPING CHALLENGE

Two neighbors lived near each other in the mountains. They were quite competitive and always testing each other's strength. One day, the first neighbor challenged the second to see who could chop the most wood in three hours. The second neighbor agreed to the challenge. The first man started out strong. As he chopped away, the second man chopped for about a half hour and then sat down for ten minutes under the shade of a large tree. The first man could not believe his neighbor's laziness. To his surprise, the second man continued to take these ten-minute breaks each hour for the duration of the contest. Finally the three hours passed. Not having paused to take even a single break, the first neighbor was sure victory was his. To his dismay, he found that the second neighbor had chopped twice as much wood as he had! In disbelief, he said, "That's impossible! You took a break every hour." Without batting an eye, the second man replied, "I wasn't resting; I was sharpening my axe."

MEANING

If we don't take the time to develop and fine-tune our core qualities (listed below), we will always lose in the end. As in sharpening the axe, we may not see the instant short-term gain from working on our core qualities, but the long-term benefits are huge. We know we should sharpen the axe (i.e., work on these skills), but who has the time, energy, desire, or focus? If you don't sharpen your axe, it will become dull and useless. When we master these core qualities, our axes are sharp, and we develop charisma at a much faster rate.

CORE QUALITIES SKILLS/TRAITS

- Self-discipline
- Competence
- Intuition
- Purpose
- Integrity
- Courage
- Creativity
- Focus

CHAPTER 8

SELF-DISCIPLINE:
WILLPOWER EQUALS COMMITMENT

In reading the lives of great men, I found that the first victory
they won was over themselves . . . self-discipline with all of
them came first.

— HARRY S. TRUMAN

When we hear the words *self-discipline* or *willpower*, we tend to get a little tense. We think of all our bad habits, things we don't want to do, or all the times we tried to exercise willpower and failed. Self-discipline is a critical life skill we need to develop to be charismatic and highly influential in the long term. Sure you can have some charisma without discipline, but lacking self-discipline will slowly erode your ability to influence others, especially when they see your weaknesses. An old saying is that, in life, you will either be disciplined or you will be disappointed.

Discipline and willpower are also known as inner strength. This strength is what drives and motivates us to achieve true success. It keeps us going in the right direction and helps us find courage and persistence. We tend to tune out the topics of discipline and will-power because we don't want to feel uneasy. Watching TV is easier than reading a book; picking up fast food is easier than eating a healthy diet; staying broke is easier than becoming financially independent. People want results now—instant gratification—and when they don't get them right away, they give up or say they can't do it. Well, look around you: Self-discipline works, and it will work for you if you make the effort. When you lack discipline in life, you feel lazy, uninspired, and often depressed. Those feelings are the exact opposite of how a charismatic person feels.

Discipline is a choice we make because the envisioned future results are better than our current condition. We can truly be happy in life only when we are accomplishing what we want and know we are capable of achieving. To reach the top, we must practice self-discipline all the time. We can't say, "I've been good this week, so I'll slack off for a couple of days." We need to learn to control our emotions, our habits, our minds, and our bodies. When we do so, we can stay committed even when we don't feel like it, our mood has gone south, or are experiencing negative emotions. This mental posture not only attracts different people to you, but gives you peace, increased motivation, and massive success.

Self-discipline is like a willpower battery. As you exercise your discipline throughout the day, the battery's energy (willpower) declines. What drains your battery? Fatigue, resisting temptations, negative emotions, low blood sugar, suppression of emotions, and even peer pressure will drain your willpower battery faster than anything else. The more we sequentially exercise our self-discipline, the more we drain our battery. Charismatic people seem to have more drive and self-discipline. They will have days when their willpower is low, but they have a game plan to charge it up. What works for you? Humor, a nap, meditation, exercise, visualization, or doing something you're good at. You must create a game plan to be aware that your discipline is low and decide how you are going to recharge that battery before the charge runs out.

Many of your habits are so deeply ingrained that it will take you time and energy to make the change. Successful people understand that changes will come only when they acknowledge their bad habits. They admit to themselves that they need to change, and they find the discipline to make the change happen. Discipline brings courage and confidence, which magnifies your charisma. I know you can't be 100 percent self-disciplined every minute of every day, but you can strengthen your future self-discipline every day. Your life is an accumulation of all your habits. Your day-to-day behavior and results are always tied into your habits. Take a look at your habits, and acknowledge any bad habits you have. Charismatic people have discovered their weak habits and made the necessary changes.

BLIND SPOT

Obviously, if you don't have self-discipline, you can't really ask others to be disciplined. The big blind spot is that being disciplined in one aspect of your life does not mean that you have self-discipline. The lack of discipline in all aspects of your life will pull you down. Let's say you are disciplined in four areas of your life, but in two other areas you are not so disciplined. Each weak area of your life affects the strong areas of your life. Self-discipline is critical in every aspect of your life. Be careful with this blind spot. Most people rate their self-discipline much higher than it actually is. This misperception causes them to never address the major weaknesses in their lives.

APPLICATION

What can you do to strengthen your willpower and your self-discipline? Doing so is easier than you think. You already have the desire, and you already know you are capable of more. You know you want more success in your life. This is what you can do to enhance your self-discipline:

- Break your goals down into smaller steps or smaller pieces.
- Visualize what you are going to get rather than what you are giving up.
- Monitor your progress on an hourly or daily basis.
- Make sure your objective is really what you want.
- Recruit friends to help support you on your path to success.

- Mentally prepare yourself that you might have a few setbacks.
- Have a game plan when your willpower is drained and needs to be recharged.

EXAMPLE

One of the greatest inventors in history was Thomas Alva Edison. When we think of self-discipline and sticking to a task we always think of Thomas Edison. There are many stories about Edison's failing thousands of times in trying to develop the electric light bulb. Sources say he never claimed those as failures, but as successful attempts at finding things that would not work. His ability to overcome setbacks and his quest for perfection are obvious parts of his success. He was so focused on what he wanted that his self-discipline became a natural part of who he was and what he accomplished. He was one of the most prolific inventors in history. He had 1,093 U.S. patents, which include the phonograph, the motion picture camera, and, of course, the light bulb.

CHARISMA KEY

The key to self-discipline is to understand how your habits are helping or hurting you. What can you do to develop healthier habits and a stronger self-discipline? Choose the one habit that is really holding you back from achieving your objectives. Ask yourself, where are your habits taking you? Then ponder the long-term consequences of the habit. Come up with a game plan for replacing the habit and for what are you going to do when your self-discipline weakens. Choose your weakest habit today, find your solution, and create a game plan.

Rate Your Self-Discipline
Add your score to page 182.

0	1	2	3	4	5	6	7	8	9	10
Poor		*Weak*			*Average*		*Strong*			*Perfect*

CHAPTER 9

COMPETENCE:
WHAT YOU DON'T KNOW WILL HURT YOU

We must believe in ourselves or no one else will believe in us;
we must match our aspirations with the competence, courage,
and determination to succeed.

— ROSALYN SUSSMAN

A critical ingredient to radiating charisma and enhancing your ability to influence others is to have comprehensive competence, knowledge, or expertise in the area where others expect you to have it. Being a role model is hard if your audience thinks that you have no idea what you are talking about or don't have the needed or perceived abilities. If they have not seen (or heard) you do what you are asking them to do, they are less willing to let you take the lead. Rebellion and resentment result when you ask others to do things they know you aren't willing to do yourself. True charismatic people model the correct way to do what they want others to do.

You have to set the standard and be the example of competence before you become truly influential.

Competence consists of your knowledge and capability in your field. Competence comes from lifelong learning and experience. When people are observing you, they subconsciously assign you a certain level of competency. Can you really do what others expect of you? Can you deliver what you promise? Does your audience think you have the skills, the talent, the knowledge, and the resources? They will find out eventually. Become and remain an expert in your field. One way to keep your competency on track is to be a continuous learner. Competence is also learning from your mistakes and always using experience as a future tool of your expertise. Become the best in your field. Make it obvious you are beyond proficient.

You've heard it before and you know it is true: Knowledge is power. Your knowledge is based on your expertise on a certain topic, system, or situation. Having more knowledge or expertise than your audience enhances your charisma. For example, lawyers, mechanics, and pharmacists possess knowledge power. We rely on these professionals' opinions, believe what they say, and trust them because of the training or experience they bring to their fields. Competence increases when you know something your audience needs to know—such as facts, information, or data—or have access to resources—such as people, property, goods, or even services—that are valued by others. Are you perceived as having the right affiliations? What connections do you have?

Passion is a great thing to have, but without the perception of competence you cannot radiate charisma or influence anyone. True competence is when you combine your ability, capabilities, and skills. Having competence increases your expertise, enhances charisma, and commands respect from your audience.

BLIND SPOT

Even if you were once at the top of your game, and even if now you have talent and intelligence, you are not necessarily perceived as competent. How *are* you perceived? Think about it. Are you sure about your answer? You should know more about your subject than 99 percent of the population. You must have a constant training and improvement program, no matter how much you think you know. You have to keep yourself aware of changes or improvements in your industry, so that you always possess cutting-edge information. You will quickly lose your competence and influence when your audience detects that they are more knowledgeable than you. All competence erodes over time and becomes obsolete. What have you learned today?

APPLICATION

You can increase your competence and others' perception of your competence in a number of ways:

- Have someone endorse you or explain your qualifications.
- Make sure your office and external surroundings radiate competence.
- Keep your reputation untarnished.
- Get others to refer you.
- Degrees, accreditation, and titles help with initial competence.
- Always have a definite opinion about your area of expertise.

EXAMPLE

Fred Smith, founder and CEO of FedEx, is a great example of competence. He built FedEx from the ground to a company that makes over $37 billion a year and employs over 140,000 people. Smith is a big believer in constant learning and education. He endorses taking the time and exerting the effort to always be learning and growing; he also believes that everyone should study and learn the many lessons that history can teach us. As a continuous learner, Smith created a multibillion-dollar company in a new industry by creating a network through a central hub. By having true competence, he created a demand for a new service that everyone today must have.

CHARISMA KEY

The key to developing competence is patience. Nothing works perfectly the first time we learn it or try it. Sometimes competence takes time to surface. The reality is that we are all incompetent in everything until we make ourselves competent. Keep focused and keep learning until you feel you can demonstrate competence in your field. Know that short-term setbacks are a part of long-term success. Remember the historical examples of Abe Lincoln, Thomas Edison, and Winston Churchill. Their early failures led to eventual success.

Another key is to become educated and informed in topics outside your expertise. This can be beneficial in connecting, building rapport, and building future relationships.

Rate Your Competence
Add your score to page 182.

0	1	2	3	4	5	6	7	8	9	10
Poor		*Weak*			*Average*			*Strong*		*Perfect*

CHAPTER 10

INTUITION:
FOLLOW YOUR INSTINCT

Often you have to rely on intuition.

— BILL GATES

Whether you call it a hunch, a gut reaction, or just a feeling, intuition is real and can be harnessed to increase your ability to influence and transmit charisma. Intuition helps you read and understand people in an instant. Intuition is a combination of your feelings, your wisdom, and your experience. People who are able to distinguish between random thoughts and intuition are more successful in life and in business. CEOs of large corporations, for example, have access to all the research they need to make sound, educated decisions. Yet the successful ones will admit that ultimately they have to follow their heart and use personal intuition.

When we pay attention to our instincts, we have the ability to read people from facial expressions, gestures, or tone of voice. This ability comes from our early programming as humans to be able to meet others and instantly decide whether they are friend or foe. Those with the ability to follow their intuition correctly were able to sense danger or make a new friend. Nowadays, when we meet someone, we usually have categorized them within the first 30 seconds. We have decided whether we like or dislike the person; this judgment comes from our intuition.

Of course, research is important. You should spend time gathering and analyzing information, but you can keep gathering information for the rest of your life. At some point you will have to make a decision, and you should let your intuition guide you. This will take a little faith and a little practice. Learn to stretch yourself. Don't limit yourself to the facts or to the opinions of other people. You have to learn to follow your heart and tap into your priceless intuition.

Some of us are afraid to talk about intuition because it is so hard to explain. Let me assure you that successful people use it every day. They don't always openly talk about it, but they are using it because intuition is more valuable than you realize. They use it to enhance their creativity, charisma, and ability to connect with others. Sure, superanalytical people tend to shoot down intuition as "woo-woo" concept or just a myth, but it is a skill you can learn and master. Not understanding how something works does not mean that it doesn't work.

Intuition expands our ability to tap into our previous experience, our knowledge, and our stored memories. We might not remember what memories or experience we are drawing on, but something we already have learned is expressed as a gut feeling. The main obstacle that blocks us from following our intuition is convincing ourselves that it works and that it should be taken seriously. It might manifest as an impulse, an urge, or even an inner voice. We are always receiving information through our intuition. We just need to listen. How does your intuition talk to you? What are you listening for? Start listening, and you will save yourself a lot of time, energy, and money.

Our instincts can evaluate our previous experiences, sense the emotions of the moment, and rely on past knowledge. As you practice using your intuition, new and inspiring ideas will instinctively arise on their own. You will be able to solve problems faster. Learn to focus and concentrate; this type of focus will nurture and augment your newfound inner strength and instinct. Your logical mind will fight you on these new thoughts and ideas, but eventually your intuition will win.

Thoughts also diminish your ability to listen to your intuition. Part of harnessing your intuition is your ability to control your thoughts. Highly influential and charismatic people have mastered the ability to control and direct their thoughts. They have the ability to focus more on positive thoughts than on negative ones. Finding your inner voice and your intuition gives you the courage, the confidence, and the insight to do or face anything.

Take a realistic look at your life right now. Are you where you want to be? Where you are is the sum total of your thoughts over the course of a lifetime. Your thoughts program your subconscious mind, which helps you use your intuition. Control of your thoughts might come in an instant, or it might take a few days, weeks, or even longer. Nevertheless, your subconscious mind will continue working on a solution. Charismatic people work on this mental training every day, while most people ignore the great potential—thinking they've heard it all before.

BLIND SPOT

We have all heard about the power of intuition. There is a direct correlation between your ability to make sound quick decisions and your success. Our blind spot is that we second-guess ourselves or that we don't even try to listen to our instincts. The first challenge is that perhaps we have tried listening to our instincts a few times, but it did not work for us; so we become a little gun-shy. Because it didn't work once, we think that it will never work. The second challenge is that intuition sounds a little hokey. We ask ourselves, "Can it really be that easy?" Or we think it works for other people, but not for us. Believe me, intuition works and is part of your core foundation of charisma.

APPLICATION

Four steps will help you tune into your inner voice and your instincts:

1. *Take time to be alone with your thoughts.* Clear your mind, and learn to focus on the moment so that external noise and internal dialog don't drown out your inner voice.
2. *Watch your attitude.* Attitude comes from your expectations. Learn to expect with confidence that your intuition will lead and guide you to the right decisions.
3. *Listen and comply.* When you get that feeling, instinct, or impulse, act on it. You might not understand it, but follow the voice and learn how it communicates with you.
4. *Practice and perfect.* Learning to master your intuition will take time, energy, and practice. Start with the small things and build up the use of your intuition.

EXAMPLE

Walt Disney had the insight and intuition to build Disneyland. He had a gut feeling that a unique amusement park based on his company's creations would appeal to both children and adults. Along the way were thousands of reasons to quit and hundreds of people who told him to give up, but he followed his instinct and listened to his internal voice, not to the criticisms of others. Disneyland was a resounding success and led to other Disney amusement parks, such as Disney World. Later on, Disney was driven and inspired to build EPCOT (Experimental Prototype Community of Tomorrow), a park dedicated to international culture and technological innovation. Everyone told him not to do it, reciting the long list of reasons why it was not a good idea (just as people said about Disneyland). But he had the dream, he felt it was the right thing to do, and he had the courage and willpower to pursue it. Disney could have taken the easy route and given in to his critics, but his intuition told him to keep going—and he did.

CHARISMA KEY

The easiest way to master intuition is to choose a time during the day (morning is usually the best) to think about and ponder your biggest challenges. Learn to listen to your thoughts, follow your instinct, and solve your challenge. As you obtain more experience and learn to listen to your intuition and trust your instinct, the process will become easier and feel more natural to you. Keep an open mind and practice these skills. Find the process and techniques that work best for you. Learn from the simple answers for which you can receive immediate feedback and know how well the process is working. Track your results, practice today, and fine-tune your ability to listen to your intuition.

Rate Your Intuition
Add your score to page 182.

0	1	2	3	4	5	6	7	8	9	10
Poor		*Weak*			*Average*		*Strong*			*Perfect*

CHAPTER 11

PURPOSE:
TAPPING INTO UNLIMITED DRIVE

When you discover your mission, you will feel its demand. It will fill you with enthusiasm and a burning desire to get to work on it.

—**W. Clement Stone**

Many people confuse emotion with purpose. Your emotions will constantly change. When you have true purpose, not only do you attract more people and become more influential, but your purpose drives them. Purpose causes you to ooze charisma. Leading and influencing others is very difficult when you have no direction yourself. We all have greatness in us, as well as the ability to design our life. I believe that each of us has within us unwritten books, unstarted businesses, brilliant ideas, great inventions, charitable ideas, and great causes to support. Yet most people have a hard time knowing how to identify their purpose. What is your purpose?

What is your destiny? Where do your interests and gifts and talents lie? What is your mission in life?

Some people may feel that daily affirmations will force their purpose on the universe and cause their dreams to come true. Popular books suggest that, if you believe and want something enough, the universe will reward you. I agree that affirmations and attraction are part of the formula to success and tapping into your purpose, but there is a lot more to the formula. Affirmations can help you in the long run, but they must be coupled with a game plan and with concrete knowledge and skills.

When you tap into that purpose, life gets easier and more fun. You will find getting up in the morning something to look forward to and never to dread. When you create your purpose, make sure you dream big and find something that not only excites you but stretches you too. Don't be discouraged if your purpose doesn't manifest itself immediately. You can make excuses and rationalize all day why you are not pursuing your passion, but you will not be happy or reach the success you are capable of achieving until you find and follow your true purpose. You must decide that you want to be in the game, that you want to enjoy the victories as well as suffer the bruises and defeats. You are in charge of your life. How you live it is your decision and yours alone.

A word of caution: As you pursue your purpose, some people in this world will pull you down, ridicule your dreams, and diminish your ideas. They'll tell you that it's impractical, improbable, or irresponsible. When you tell others about your purpose, revealing to them the things you want to accomplish in life, many people tend to be discouraging. What they think or say doesn't matter. Every person of influence, success, and charisma has countless stories about people who told them their ideas would not work. However, tapping into your purpose will unleash within you your greatest energy and imagination. And just like striking oil, you will experience a surge of greater productivity than you have ever had in your life.

BLIND SPOT

Society nurtures a great blind spot in us when we try to understand our true purpose and potential. Most people have never really

found or discovered their purpose in life. In life we are either working for our own goals or somebody else's goals. We tend to borrow
our goals, rent our dreams, and lease our purpose from others and
from society. True influence and charisma come when you have
found your purpose and your passion and when others see that fire
in your eyes. When you achieve charisma, others will be attracted
to your purpose and assimilate it. It is time for you to tap into your
purpose.

APPLICATION

Do you know your purpose? Do you want to know exactly what
greatness lies within you? Do you want to get a better feel for the
direction you should take in life? Give these questions some continuous thought and meditation. The answers might come right away,
or they might take days, weeks, or even months to reveal themselves. Answer the following questions:

- If you knew you would succeed—if you knew you could not
  fail—what would you do if you were guaranteed success?
  What would you try? What would you become?

- If you could magically and instantly change one thing in the
  world, what would it be? What would you change?

- Imagine you became financially independent and no longer
  had to work, no longer had to think about making money
  and paying bills. What would you do with your time? How
  would you spend your day?

EXAMPLE

The definition of tapping into and magnifying your purpose is em-
bodied in Dr. Martin Luther King Jr. His life and his mission
changed the lives of millions of people. Once he was committed to
his mission, he knew where he was going and what he was destined
to do, regardless of the consequences. On April 3, 1968, Martin Luther King gave his famous address, "I've Been to the Mountaintop,"

in Memphis, Tennessee. Before he started speaking, he received a threat against his life. In his speech he said, "We've got some difficult days ahead. But it doesn't matter with me now. Because I've been to the mountaintop. And I don't mind. Like anybody, I would like to live a long life. Longevity has its place. But I'm not concerned about that now. I just want to do God's will. And He's allowed me to go up to the mountain. And I've looked over. And I've seen the promised land. I may not get there with you. But I want you to know tonight, that we, as a people will get to the promised land. And I'm happy, tonight. I'm not worried about anything. I'm not fearing any man. Mine eyes have seen the glory of the coming of the Lord." This historic speech revealed his destiny. He had found and tapped into his purpose. His prophecy came true when he was assassinated the next day outside his motel room.

CHARISMA KEY

As you tap into and retune your purpose in life, you may face some turbulence. At times the universe will test you to see whether your purpose is a faint hope or a true burning desire. The key is to look at every obstacle or challenge in your way as getting one step closer to fulfilling your purpose. Do these challenges make you a better person or a bitter person? I believe that every challenge or obstacle you face in life can become a learning experience that you can use to take your life or success to the next level. When these defining moments hit, they can either give you constant mental pain or enable you to tap into your purpose. Today when faced with a challenge, confront it with optimism and ask yourself, "What do I need to learn?"

Rate Your Purpose
Add your score to page 182.

0	1	2	3	4	5	6	7	8	9	10
Poor		*Weak*			*Average*		*Strong*			*Perfect*

CHAPTER 12

INTEGRITY:
CHARACTER COUNTS

The most important persuasion tool you have in your entire arsenal is integrity.

—Zig Ziglar

The world *integrity* comes from the Latin word *integritas*. It means purity, correctness, soundness, and blamelessness. It can also be defined as consistency between your values and actions, between what you believe and what you actually do. When you want to influence others and enhance your charisma, you must radiate integrity. People must know and feel that you believe what you say and will do what you say. We want to be around people we know are honest, sincere, and genuine. The first part of tapping into your integrity is knowing yourself, knowing your values, and knowing exactly what you stand for.

What do you really believe in, and what are you willing to stand up for? Do you have a strong personal conviction that dictates all the decisions you make? When you radiate integrity, people know your values and beliefs. At times we are faced with a conflict between our beliefs and desires. Our integrity then dictates which one is right and therefore which one will succeed. Pure integrity helps you establish the ground rules before things get tense or emotional. It determines who you are and how you will respond to a given situation before it happens.

The moment of influence is tarnished when no one knows where you stand or what you believe. This creates conflict, indecision, and resistance. Creating a perception of integrity does not happen overnight; it is not recognized in an instant by those you attempt to influence. It is a combination of your history, your honesty, your fairness, and your unimpaired judgment. The challenge with integrity is that it takes time to build and seconds to lose.

Having great integrity is also part of your character. Character is made up of such qualities as honesty, sincerity, and predictability. I consider solid character and integrity to be the very foundation of one's ability to succeed. No success is going to be great or lasting if it stems from questionable ethics, motives, or behaviors. Even if you are an honest person of great character, it is human nature for people to cast sweeping judgments and formulate opinions without all the facts. So, if you want genuine trust and lasting integrity, you must avoid even the appearance of anything that might be considered untruthful or unethical.

Isn't it interesting to see so many corporate mission statements containing the word *integrity* and yet so many of these companies brought down by the lack of it? Usually, what brings these companies down isn't the action of outside market forces but the lack of integrity on the inside. One historical example is the Great Wall of China. The people wanted to feel safe; they wanted security. So they built a wall so big and so impressive that no one could climb over it. It was impenetrable and no one could smash it down. This Great Wall was 4,000 miles long, up to 25 feet high and 15 to 30 feet wide. But during the first 100 years of the Wall's existence, it failed to keep out China's enemies. What was going on? It was the lack of integrity of the people inside the Wall. The gatekeepers were bribed to let in the enemies, who marched right through without meeting any resistance.

BLIND SPOT

Creating a perception of integrity tends to be a challenge for many people because most don't realize how they are coming across to others. They feel they have enough integrity and are doing okay. Or they might think others should have integrity, but cutting corners here and there is no big deal. When you think this way, it will erode your personal foundation of integrity. To be charismatic, you must tap into that internal guidance system that navigates you correctly through every situation. It is a compass that will guide your thoughts and your feelings based on integrity. Making decisions and choosing a direction are so much easier when you have a foundation of integrity, know what you believe, and are willing to stand up for your beliefs and values.

APPLICATION

What are your values? What do you really believe in? Tapping into your values will increase your passion, your integrity, and your ability to influence other people. You cannot influence or inspire others if you do not know your own values and are therefore unable to share them with others. Here are some tips to help you tap into and discover your values and how to live by those values:

- Write down your definition of a value.
- Take time to ponder and reflect on your true beliefs.
- Find people you respect and define their values.
- Find people in history you admire, and determine whether their values are your values.
- Live up to everything you say you are going to do.
- Tell the truth even though it hurts.

EXAMPLE

A great example of integrity is Mitt Romney. He is credited with saving the 2002 Winter Olympics. First of all, he turned around what had been a growing fiscal crisis and made the 2002 games a financial success. Perhaps more important, he restored the damaged reputation of the United States Olympic organization. The previous Olympic committee had been scarred by bribery and ethics complaints. Unethical things had happened, which began to destroy the credibility of the Olympic Games. Americans were angry; many said they would not even watch the Winter Games on TV. Mitt Romney was called in to save the day. His integrity and honesty turned the games around. He was open, forthright, and unbending in his values. He did not try to hide or cover up anything that had happened. As a result, the American people felt he was being honest with them and sensed his integrity. He was able to restore the confidence in the Games and in the Olympic committee.

CHARISMA KEY

Today (and every day), do what you say you are going to do. Integrity is not something you need to announce or broadcast. When so-called religious people have to announce how religious they are, we know to watch out. If you make promises to others, learn to keep them even if they seem minor to you; they might be major to other people. Own up to your mistakes or errors. You do not have to be perfect, but have the character and integrity to try. People appreciate your honesty about your mistakes and weaknesses—they see them, even if they don't call you on them. Today admit a past (or present) mistake and watch the respect increase and your sense of integrity soar.

Rate Your Integrity
Add your score to page 182.

0	1	2	3	4	5	6	7	8	9	10
Poor		*Weak*			*Average*		*Strong*			*Perfect*

Add your score to page 182.

CHAPTER 13

COURAGE:

STAND UP AND BE COUNTED

You have to risk losing the race to win it.

— **Lance Armstrong**

The Latin root of the word *courage* means heart, bravery, will, and spirit. You know when your find your purpose that you must have the courage to pursue it. Part of courage is following your heart, knowing you are on the right track, even though at times you might stray off the track and hit a tree. Overall, you know you're heading in the right direction regardless of minor setbacks. I love what Aristotle said about courage: "Courage is the first human virtue because it makes all of the other virtues possible." Most of the time we think of courage when there are threats or the possibility of physical harm. Facing an individual threat may take courage, but courage is a daily attribute needed to influence others to your point of view. People need to know you have the courage and heart to do the things you say you are going to do even if things get rough. Courage is part of your charisma.

There is courage in not trying to be nice all the time and starting to call people on their weaknesses and challenges. You need courage to correct someone or to start that uncomfortable and awkward conversation. You need courage to have the confrontation when you know it would be easier not to and just hope the problem will go away. Helping someone in a time of need when it is not convenient for you is another form of courage. Truly charismatic people will take those risks; they will venture into the unknown and tackle the challenges everyone else hopes will go away. Others always know that such people will have the courage to do what is needed and what is right.

Having courage (or being brave) does not mean you don't feel fear. It just means you have the heart and emotional stability to face the fear and do what's needed anyway. This is a process of learning about yourself—who you are and what you are able to do. Identifying your weaknesses, changing your habits, and fixing your attitude all require personal bravery. Courage is about helping yourself and helping other people become better, knowing as you grow and help others grow that you could be subject to criticism. It is not fun to face our fears. We don't want to open ourselves up for failure, but this is where our courage comes in. Fear and failure are all part of your success and influencing others to be more successful. When you develop this inner strength, you acknowledge your fear and the possibility of failure, and you stay on track.

Facing fear could mean stepping up to the plate and making the tough decision. You gain respect from everyone when you can make those tough decisions. This brand of courage breeds conviction that will allow you to keep going even when times are rough. I am not talking about being stubborn. Part of courage, at times, is admitting you were wrong and moving forward.

You need to find the heart, courage, and strength to do two things. First, stop blaming other people. Not blaming others enhances your courage. Sure, blaming someone else is easy, but the reality is that now is the time to take full ownership. If you can place the blame on other people, events, or circumstances, you can relieve yourself of the shame and guilt. Don't delude yourself with the apparent comfort that laying blame is going to make things better. Take full responsibility for every part of your life, and courage will develop.

Second, accept failure. How you handle setbacks and failures will make or break you. When you know you can handle anything—even failure—you will develop unlimited courage. When you are following your heart and have tapped into your purpose, then a little failure will have no effect. There is a big difference between failing and being a failure. A failure results from not learning from your mistakes and from not using that valuable education to invest in your future. Negative and bad things will happen to you; the benefit is in how you deal with those turns of events. What will you learn from those experiences? How can you use them to develop greater courage?

BLIND SPOT

It has been said that the early explorers got the arrows. Some people want others to have courage and take the arrows, but they want the credit for the discovery or the victory. Courage is knowing you will fail a few times before the victory, and that is okay. Learn to take the arrows on the path to victory. The blind spot is not understanding that winning is all about losing. The blind spot is not being willing to try new things because you might fail. When you lose or suffer a setback, you need courage to keep going. Courage is essential to propel you forward after the sting of defeat. You should realize every time you lose or face a setback that you are closer to victory. A temporary failure does not make you a permanent failure.

APPLICATION

How do you apply courage? How do you learn to follow your heart? How do you do what you are supposed to do, when you don't feel like doing it and when fear is staring you in the face? Here are some pointers:

- ❧ Remember the times you have been courageous and did the right thing.

- Think about your strengths and past accomplishments.

- Learn to take small risks and ask yourself, "What's the worst that could happen?"

- Spend time on your visualization. When you can see yourself doing it, it is easier to do it.

- Watch how others exhibit courage and tackle the tough problems.

- Know when it is time to ask for help.

- After every setback or failure, ask yourself, "What did I do well and what could I do better?"

EXAMPLE

There are many sad examples of not having the courage to stand up and do what is right. Countless people have not had the courage to pursue their dreams, or they have given up too fast. Think of all the people you know who have had dreams, aspirations, and goals, and you saw their passion wither away until it was gone. Orville and Wilbur Wright had the courage to dream, the heart to pursue that dream, and the guts to put up with public ridicule. Even after a failed flight experiment (which many witnessed), Orville wrote, "I do not know if heavier than air flight is possible. But, I choose to live my life dedicated to the idea that it is." The rest is history. They had the courage to do what they felt they wanted and needed to do. These brothers changed the world of travel forever by having the courage to follow their heart.

CHARISMA KEY

Talking about courage and wanting to have courage is all great, but what can we do to find and maintain a constant level of courage? What are you going to do with all these fears rattling around in your psyche? What fear is holding you back? Fear and a lack of courage do not breed charisma. Don't allow yourself to be immobilized by past mistakes. You are better off for the knowledge and experience you have gained from them. How do you unlearn a long-time fear, an experience in the past that holds you hostage? You must face it. That's right: You must deliberately put yourself into the situation where you are confronted with your fear and there is no escape. The courage comes from the reality that, when you face your fear, it really isn't that bad. Remember most of our fears are exaggerated doubts or based on unrealistic perceptions.

I want you to choose one fear right now that is holding you back and face it today. Face the fear, free yourself from your bondage, and develop true contagious courage.

Rate Your Courage
Add your score to page 182.

0	1	2	3	4	5	6	7	8	9	10
Poor		*Weak*			*Average*		*Strong*		*Perfect*	

CHAPTER 14

CREATIVITY:
TAP YOUR IMAGINATION

Imagination is more important than knowledge.
—ALBERT EINSTEIN

No one can really go far in life without tapping into his or her own internal creativity. Most people underestimate both their own creative potential and that of those around them. As a charismatic person, you must be able to collectively join and unite creative forces to solve challenges. What is creativity? It is being resourceful and imaginative. It is the ability to generate new ideas to solve old or new problems. When you have tapped into your creativity, you can find new ways and practices to improve existing systems. When you tap into the creativity of those around you, you generate new interest in your goals and more excitement about the future.

Being creative is taking old ideas, new ideas, and imagination and creating a combination that solves a problem. It consists of taking thoughts or ideas that may seem unrelated and formulating a creative solution. Everyone has access to the same information, but creativity blooms when people see, organize, or combine the information in new ways. One thing that holds people back is their focus on all the negative aspects of the problem they are trying to solve. They focus so much on worrying about what could go wrong that they miss the solution or what could go right. Creativity is a right-brained activity. If you can dream, if you can imagine, if you can hope, you can be creative.

When you can tap into your creativity or allow those around you to feel open to being creative, then you have opened the doors to creative solutions. You become more charismatic. You and the people around you will collectively find the right answers, and often those answers could not be found by one individual person. People who tend to be more creative are more successful, more open to change, and see opportunity even in the greatest of setbacks. They can think of new possibilities, feel more in control, and spend more time on the results versus the problem. Creative people are all around you. Your job as a charismatic person is to become creative yourself and to empower others to be creative and help them feel safe with their creativity.

Tapping into your creativity does not mean that all of a sudden you will be doing excellent work or solving all the world's problems. Creativity is more like the spark that ignites the fire. The willingness to be wrong, the desire to experiment, and having the courage to fail are all ingredients you will need to maintain your creativity. Part of being creative is never being satisfied with the status quo; it is the willingness to ask "why" at the right times. You must create an atmosphere for creativity. Don't downplay any ideas, and always show enthusiasm for new ideas and the willingness of others to think innovatively.

Many resist being creative because they don't want to rock the boat. They question their ideas: "What if it doesn't work?" We all want guarantees that our plans will work. We want to see the results or know what others think before we make a comment or suggestion. But to win the game, we have to pay the price and face the consequences. When you are creative and stick your neck out, you will hit bumps in the road, but you'll never get to your destination if you aren't willing to get past those bumps. Top performers know that creative change is the key to their success, to their ability to influence others, and to creating long-term charisma.

BLIND SPOT

The self-perception bias with creativity comes with the mind-numbing thoughts that "I'm not creative." or that creativity cannot be learned. Creativity is like every skill and attribute in this book; everyone can learn and master each one of them. It does not matter if you have tried to be creative in the past. Try again and try harder this time. Creativity will open your mind, you will feel less tied down, and you will see more solutions. Whether you tend to compare yourself to highly creative people or hope to be more creative does not matter. Creativity does not spring from a magic brain region that some people have and others don't. The skill can be learned. Learn to trust your mind for creative solutions.

APPLICATION

Here are six steps you can follow to become more creative right now.

1. *Always try to find at least five solutions to each challenge.* This effort forces you to be creative and to understand that there is not always one solution to every challenge.
2. *Use group synergy and energy to find solutions.* Other people's experience, education, and thinking processes are different and should be used.
3. *Never downplay any suggestions or ideas.* Sure, some suggestions might be less than ideal, but as a group you can build, change, adjust, or fine-tune any idea to solve your challenge.
4. *Have confidence in your subconscious mind.* Many of the answers are there. Take time to be alone with your thoughts and trust in yourself that the answers will come to the surface.
5. *Practice telling stories, metaphors, or analogies.* Choose any subject at random, and come up with various ways to teach

someone else the topic using stories, metaphors, or analogies. This exercises your creative muscle.

6. *Be patient with the solution you are seeking.* It might take longer than expected, but the perfect solution is always worth the wait.

EXAMPLE

Henry Ford is a great example of creativity. He was always the one to shake things up and think of things or procedures that were not generally accepted. He had a very lively imagination (sometimes even strange) and was known to daydream. He was an incredible inventor with 161 U.S. patents. He changed the concept of a factory when he created the assembly line for making his automobiles. He was able to produce cars at record speeds, which meant lower prices and more profit. He paid his workers well, enabling them to buy his cars and generating incredible loyalty. His creativity forever changed a nation, changed an industry, and changed manufacturing.

CHARISMA KEY

Creativity involves the ability to generate new ideas. To master creativity, you must have access to new information. Read new books, listen to educational CDs, watch the Discovery Channel, pick a foreign topic to review or learn, and so on. Branch out and learn from many different industries and topics. Magazines can be a great resource to stimulate your mind. Hang out with children. They are naturally creative and will expand your creativity. Your mind will become more fertile and more imaginative, and you will be able to generate new creative ideas when you need them. Today, I want you to brainstorm ten creative ideas to solve your biggest challenge.

Rate Your Creativity
Add your score to page 182.

0	1	2	3	4	5	6	7	8	9	10
Poor		*Weak*			*Average*		*Strong*		*Perfect*	

CHAPTER 15

FOCUS:
ACTIVITY DOES NOT EQUAL
ACCOMPLISHMENT

It's not enough to be busy; so are the ants.

— HENRY DAVID THOREAU

A big indicator of success is the ability to control impulses, resist distraction, and stay focused on the task at hand. Most people waste the majority of the day because they are unable to focus and concentrate. Influencing others is difficult if you cannot stay focused or are unable to work on the current task. If you are scatterbrained, you will come across as disorganized, and your communications will appear disjointed. Successful people do not start their day until they have created it on paper: what they will be doing, what they want to accomplish, and where the priorities lie. Preparation and goal setting are always mentioned prominently in any book on success. They help us become more organized, accomplish more, and create the ability to focus and concentrate.

We all have the same amount of time. Yet why do certain people accomplish so much more in the same amount of time? They do so for two reasons: first, focus and concentration; second, goals. You can focus much more easily when your direction and what you need to accomplish are clear and precise. Knowing what you need to do makes time management and decision making much easier. If we focus on unimportant tasks, they will fill up our day, and we will be busy, but unable to accomplish the most important things that need to be done on that day. If you need a little help with this category, ask yourself these four questions:

1. What is the best use of my time right now?
2. Am I spending vital time on unimportant things?
3. Do I confuse being busy with accomplishment?
4. Am I clear about exactly what I need to achieve?

When you look at successful people in all endeavors, you will find people who can focus and concentrate. Your ability to turn off the outside noise and focus on what you need to do, when you need to do it, not only is a great time management technique, but a critical ingredient in your success. The challenge is that we waste so much energy avoiding things we don't want to do that we become unable to do them at all. For example, you need to go to the dentist, but you don't want to go. You think about it and put it off, but the dentist visit is always in the back of your mind. Putting our mental energy into avoiding a situation consumes our physical and mental energy. By trying not to think about it, we actually focus on it more, creating a downward spiral.

When we focus our energy on things we don't want to have happen or potential obstacles, we expend all our energy on those negative things rather than focusing it on what needs to be done now. When you can concentrate and focus on the correct things, you achieve success much faster. You will develop true charisma, and it will be easier to influence others. Forget your past mistakes, and learn to concentrate on your future potential. Sure, it takes some mental energy and exertion, but the effort is a critical life skill.

We want to hide the past and forget our shortcomings, but it is time to take ownership of them, learn from them, and get ready to master the future. When we can take an honest look at ourselves, readjusting our mental settings, then and only then can we learn to truly concentrate. We tend to turn our minds off from subjects and topics that make us feel uncomfortable. But when we are in this state of denial, nothing can change. When we recognize and face the problems of the past, we can find peace in the future. The stronger the peace, the easier it is to focus and concentrate.

BLIND SPOT

Being busy all day long does not mean we are accomplishing anything important. You have had plenty of days where you felt very busy—constantly moving—but, when you looked back on the day, you realized you had accomplished next to nothing. Our two blind spots are not seeing two key facts:

- *Activity does not mean achievement.* We waste time trying to finish a 30-minute task in three hours. We look and feel busy, but we lack a true focus.
- *We don't focus on the task at hand.* When concentration is low, at work we think about being at home, and at home we are thinking about work. Wherever you are, make sure you are there mentally.

APPLICATION

Charismatic people have the ability to focus quickly in the moment, as great athletes do. To master the area of focus and concentration, you must do what athletes do before, during, and after the competition.

- Visualize the win or the outcome before it happens.
- Maintain constant self-discipline even when it hurts.
- Refocus after failure and learn from mistakes.
- Instantly replace negative thoughts with positive ones.

- Have the ability to quickly change your state of mind.
- Learn to concentrate in the face of heavy distractions.

EXAMPLE

Michael Jordan's focus enabled him to maximize his talents, skills, and strengths. He is one of the greatest basketball players, if not the greatest player, of all time. He won the NBA championship six times and was named the league's Most Valuable Player five times. However, he was never satisfied with his current skill level and never stopped practicing the fundamentals. He was known as one of the hardest workers in the sport, no matter how great his prior achievements. His greatness came from his ability to focus and concentrate. He never let a failure hold him back; he could return to focus in a moment's notice. Despite his numerous accomplishments, he still lost over 300 games. The interesting fact is that in 26 of those games, the team relied on him to make the winning shot and he missed it. Yet he was always ready to come back and try again. Over his career, he missed many more game-winning shots than he made. A critical part of having great focus is to bounce back after a failure and still expect success the next time.

CHARISMA KEY

The key is to begin to focus and concentrate a little at a time. Today, take two steps:

- First, try to focus and stay on a task for five minutes. Where can you go? What do you need to do to avoid distractions? As you progress with this skill, add the length of time and your ability to limit distractions.

- Second, figure out which part of the day is your most productive time: morning, afternoon, evening? This is the time when you do your most important and difficult work. Find that time when it is the easiest to concentrate and get things done. When you truly master your ability to focus, not only is it easier to influence others, you will be able to accomplish ten times more in half the amount of time.

Rate Your Focus and Concentration
Add your score to page 182.

0	1	2	3	4	5	6	7	8	9	10
Poor		*Weak*			*Average*		*Strong*			*Perfect*

CORE QUALITIES RESOURCES (LAWSOFCHARISMA.COM)

- Support articles
- Section support audio: "Permission to Win: Mental Programming for Results"
- Section worksheet

SECTION THREE

DELIVERY AND COMMUNICATION:
SPEAK WITH CONVICTION

FABLE: THE ANT AND THE GRASSHOPPER

It was a hot August day toward the end of a long summer. A grasshopper was hopping around, enjoying the heat and singing to its heart's content. The grasshopper didn't feel he had a care in the world, and he was enjoying the moment. An ant passed by the grasshopper, carrying a large piece of nut he was attempting to take back to his collective. The ant was wondering if he could solicit help from his friend the grasshopper. Before the ant could ask for help, the grasshopper suggested, "Why don't you come play with me? You're working way too hard for this fine summer day."

The ant replied, "I'm gathering food for the winter. It would be best if you started to think about what you are going to do for nourishment during the winter."

"Oh, that's so far away," the grasshopper responded, "and there is always time for things like that. Besides, look around. There's plenty of food to go around."

The ant left, disappointed in his friend, but continued to work. When the winter arrived, the grasshopper realized there was no more food outside and he had nothing stored for the winter. "I should have listened to my friend, the ant," he thought. "Now I will go hungry."

MEANING

Communication goes both ways. The grasshopper didn't listen and didn't store food for the long winter months. When you need to know something, it is often too late to learn. Critical life skills should be learned before you need them. Those who wing it, assuming they have mastered these skills, will face a cold, dark winter ahead.

On the other hand, the ant's communication skills were at fault too. Sure, he was well fed from the corn, grain, and nuts he had stored during the summer. But he was unable to convince his friend to gather food to survive the winter, even though it was for the grasshopper's own good. When you need to influence someone, it is often too late for them to be influenced.

DELIVERY AND COMMUNICATION SKILLS/TRAITS

- Presentation skills
- People skills
- Influence
- Story mastery
- Eye contact
- Listening
- Rapport

CHAPTER 16

PRESENTATION SKILLS:
EDUCATE, INSPIRE, AND ENTERTAIN

Think twice before you speak, because your words and
influence will plant the seed of either success or failure in the
mind of another.

—NAPOLEON HILL

I know you have seen it happen, at a convention, at a conference, in an office meeting, or even on TV. You have seen people who can mesmerize others with their speaking and presentation skills. From the moment they start to the minute they finish, you are captivated, mesmerized, and in tune with their message. On the flip side, you have also been bored out of your mind and wanted to pull the fire alarm to get out of a meeting or presentation. It dragged on and on, you wanted to sleep, and the presentation sucked the life right out of you.

Charismatic people have excellent communication skills that

captive, inspire, and rivet their audience. Whether on the phone, in face-to-face interactions, during group presentations, amid negotiations, and even when texting and emailing, they can articulate their message and make it come alive in your mind. They make you feel as though you're watching a movie; they have created a mental picture so strong that it feels real. These kinds of presentation skills have been described as energetic, enthusiastic, and emotional. How would you describe your presentation skills?

Have you noticed the dramatic changes that have evolved in presentations, communication, and training over the last 20 years? The focus used to be on education. Many people today are still trying to educate, and they inevitably lose their audiences. The latest research, however, is all about how to grab and keep your audience's attention. We know that people's attention spans are getting shorter and shorter. So we can no longer focus simply on educating; we must now entertain and influence. We must keep our audience's attention. We must be charismatic.

Charismatic people are able to earn and maintain the attention of their audience. You don't have to dance around or be a stand-up comedian. You do have to make sure your audience follows your message, that your words resonate with them, that they pay attention, and that they understand your message. The moment you lose their attention, you can no longer influence them, and they definitely can't feel any charisma.

You could have a great product or cause, be a sharp dresser, publish a great brochure, or even have impressive credentials. The reality is, however, that the number-one persuasion tool is you, and a big part of how you present yourself and your charisma is your ability to communicate. Long gone are the days of hoping that people will listen, or of trying to make them listen, or of expecting that the topic will compensate for your weaknesses as a presenter. Nowadays, you have to get inside your audience's minds, and you've got to get there fast. It can take only seconds before people's minds start to wander and you lose them.

The thing about a charismatic presentation is that the audience is reeled in during the first 30 seconds—the critical time for any presentation. The audience decides whether they are going to listen or snooze. A weak introduction to your presentation is going to lose your audience right away. Learn how to start from the best presenters in the business, but make sure you adapt your presentation to your own style and energy. Be prepared to handle hecklers and those who will ask the tough questions. Learn to connect on a personal and emotional level. Make sure every member of that audience feels as though you are talking directly to him or her. Practice your presentation until it becomes part of you, instead running through a slick PowerPoint or a tired outline. Manage your fear, anxiety, or nervousness so that you can radiate charisma during your presentation.

BLIND SPOT

Being able to talk or create a PowerPoint does not mean you know how to communicate, inspire, and present. Most people feel that they have above-average communication skills and average presentation skills. That's the blind spot. The reality is that they are lucky to have average communication skills and below-average presentation skills. Sure, you can give a presentation, and no one leaves the room or says anything negative. But did you really have charisma? Did they enjoy being there? Are they going to do what you want them to do? Were they just being polite while they were bored into rigor mortis? Did you influence them to your point of view? Did you influence them to do something? Charismatic people have mastered their presentation skills, yet they are constantly working on them. There is always something to fine-tune, to learn, and to improve.

APPLICATION

Do you know how your audience perceives you? Can you improve in some areas? Are you doing things that turn off or repel your audience? Take a look at this checklist to see whether you are making any of these common communication blunders:

- Speaking in a monotone
- Avoiding eye contact
- Fidgeting and displaying other annoying mannerisms

- Using vocal fillers ("uhm," "uh," "er")
- Lacking emotion or conviction
- Sounding mechanical or rehearsed
- Rushing through the presentation
- Overloading the audience with too much information
- Displaying nervousness or fear

EXAMPLE

No matter which side of the political aisle you sit on, Ronald Reagan will forever be known as The Great Communicator. He radiated passion and conviction, and he always stood for something. He could build a dream people would buy into. He could paint a picture that would get you excited for the future. His message was always simple and to the point. During his presentations, he would connect with most of the audience. During a speech, you would feel his emotion and his enthusiasm. Reagan had the ability to speak directly to one person in an audience of 10,000 and make everyone feel connected. When you watched him speak, it was like he was speaking directly to you.

CHARISMA KEY

Have you ever had a bad case of laliophobia—the fear of public speaking? As common as this problem is, there is hope in that most of our fears are not innate, but learned. This is good news because, if you can learn a fear, you can unlearn it. We normally feel a little nervousness before a presentation. Make sure you find some way to sooth your nerves. The best two ways to do that are to visualize your successful presentation and to be prepared. You may be tempted to win over the audience by revealing that you feel nervous or unprepared (apologizing in advance), but this technique usually backfires. The people in the audience don't know how you feel or how much you prepared. Why should you tell them what to start looking for? Today, discover why speaking makes you nervous and fix it. Really, what's the worst thing that could *realistically* happen during your presentation?

Rate Your Presentation Skills
Add your score to page 182.

0	1	2	3	4	5	6	7	8	9	10
Poor		*Weak*			*Average*		*Strong*			*Perfect*

CHAPTER 17

PEOPLE SKILLS:
DO THEY REALLY LIKE YOU?

The most important single ingredient in the formula of
success is knowing how to get along with people.
—THEODORE ROOSEVELT

The ability to connect with most people is critical for charisma.
Many times an attempt to gain rapport using people skills is perceived as overeagerness, trying way too hard, or insincerity. The
old-school idea of looking around someone's office to find something to talk about will usually backfire on you for two reasons.
First, the technique has been overused and abused. Second, you are
coming across as fake and disingenuous. The key is to read people
when you meet them. Find out how they want to be treated. If your
people skills work with personality A, they may not work with personality B. Learn to adjust and customize your approach.

   The ability to work with and connect with people tops the list for charismatic people. Studies consistently show that people skills are always one of the top skills needed to succeed in life and in business. We find the ability to interact with people—to be socially in tune—is decreasing and becoming even harder for the new generation. The explosion of technology makes it tempting to think that personality and the ability to deal with people are not important qualities. Surprisingly, because of this overwhelmingly technical trend, we crave personal interaction more than ever and don't even realize it. People still want to get to know you and like you before the doors of influence and persuasion are unlocked. Charisma is enhanced when people know and like us.

We connect with people who we feel are similar to us. Look at any social gathering, and you will see that those who are similar to one another tend to gather together. Audiences will connect with you when they feel you can relate to them or have something in common with them. Charisma increases when you can find similar attitudes, beliefs, or interests. We like to network and associate with those with whom we feel a bond or some commonality. You need to be able to find agreement or something in common in as many areas as possible. And you can find commonality with everyone you meet.

First impressions are crucial because they have a huge impact on our charisma. First impressions are made in only seconds of an initial interaction with someone, so we don't have time *not* to have good people skills! It takes seconds to make a lasting lifetime impression. Dale Carnegie, one of the greats in terms of understanding human nature, said, "By becoming interested in other people, you will get them to like you faster than if you spent all day trying to get them interested in you." Caring about others entails acting with consideration, politeness, and genuine concern to those around us. It means forgetting about ourselves and our busy world and caring about somebody else. You will win hearts and loyalty through compassion. You will invoke friendliness by focusing on their positives. Don't be harsh when dealing in areas where the other person is sensitive or vulnerable.

BLIND SPOT

Do you know an annoying person who rubs you the wrong way? Do you know a person whom you don't like but pretend to like? Do you know a family member who thinks she is cool, but isn't? Well, that could be you. What am I saying? Other people could be pretending to like you because that is the polite thing to do. Can you get along with different personalities? Are you sure about that? We have never completely arrived when it comes to our people skills. It is a blind spot that says we need to work on this skill every day. It is one of the most "overrated" of all critical life skills; that is, most people say they have it, but they really don't.

APPLICATION

As you enhance and fine-tune your people skills, make sure you come across as genuine. Other people will pretend to like you even when they don't. Understand that, if your influence attempts are not working, the reason is usually because they don't like you. How can you help your people skills be genuine?

- Show respect to everyone.
- Be aware of everyone around you.
- Recognize that everyone you know or meet can help you in some way.
- Be interested in them and what they do.
- Always be helpful and willing to serve.

EXAMPLE

Mother Teresa was born in 1910 and made a lasting impact on the world through her caring, her love, and her people skills. She was born in Albania and became a Roman Catholic nun. She founded the Missionaries of Charity in Calcutta, India, in 1950 and ministered to the poor and needy for 45 years. She won the Nobel Peace Prize in 1979, and, at the time of her death, she had 610 missions in 123 countries. She had incredible people skills to manage and be respected by over 4,500 nuns around the world. She treated everyone in the same way—as the most important person on Earth.

CHARISMA KEY

The key thing to work on today is to realize you are part of one big team. You have heard that the more people you help and serve, the more people there will be to help and serve you. Success is not a solo project. On this team and on the road to charisma, there is little room for self-promotion. Give credit where credit is due. Share the recognition every time you can. Realize that the human ego is very fragile and that a damaged ego is very difficult to influence. Learn to praise and appreciate others for what they do. Never assume that appropriate compensation for good work is enough. Give sincere thanks as often as possible. Make sure today you show mutual respect, and give everyone else credit for what was accomplished.

Rate Your People Skills
Add your score to page 182.

0	1	2	3	4	5	6	7	8	9	10
Poor		*Weak*			*Average*		*Strong*		*Perfect*	

CHAPTER 18

INFLUENCE:
HELP OTHERS PERSUADE THEMSELVES

When you need to persuade and influence your audience — it is too late to learn.

— KURT W. MORTENSEN

Charisma and influence go hand in hand. In other words, charisma is getting others to do what you want them to do and like doing it. People get uneasy when you talk about influence, but, just like power, influence is neutral. Some feel it can't be learned, others feel that it might get misused, and some pretend it is not that important. Influence enables you to get people to accept your ideas, to bring people together, and to make change stick. I am not talking about selling skills. I am talking about long-term sustainable change that people want to implement. There is a direct correlation between your ability to influence, your charisma, and your income.

Most people misunderstand the concept of persuasion and influence. Influence is usually undervalued and underutilized. We persuade and influence all the time in our work, with our friends and family, with strangers we encounter in our everyday lives. True influence is not forceful, devious, or manipulative. It is a truly beneficial outcome for both parties. Great confidence and power come with your ability to influence and help others make sound decisions or support a worthwhile cause.

Make no mistake: Influence can be learned. Great people of influence are not born, they are made. And you can and should master the art of influence. Understanding the theories of persuasion, motivation, and influence will create charisma. Everything you want or will want in life comes from the ability to understand people and change their minds. You must learn to gain instant influence over others and inspire them to take action. You cannot be charismatic if you can't influence others to your way of thinking. *Everyone* needs influence skills, no matter what your occupation is. We practice and use influence techniques and tactics everyday with everyone we meet! We can't get anywhere in life unless we are able to influence other human beings. Only through our dealings with others can we achieve success. No one is self-sufficient.

Most influence happens with subconscious triggers (see Section Five). Everything you do, everything you say, and how you make them feel will affect how your audience feels about you. You may be repelling people and not even know it. When people sense a hint of force, deception, hype, or selling in any of your influence attempts, you will lose your charisma.

Most people have never learned the subtle art and science of influence. Many think they have it, but they are using transparent old-school techniques that will eventually backfire on them. Audiences are tough. People have built a lot of resistance to the old style of persuading and influence; many have built a brick wall of resistance even before you've even met them. What can you do to overcome this tendency? Your influence attempts must be non-threatening and natural. Forget loud and flashy—that strategy only encourages more resistance. And most definitely forget high pressure. Not only does that solidify resistance, it closes the door to influence. When people feel they are being pressured, bullied, or coerced into doing something they don't need or want, they become rebellious and resentful.

BLIND SPOT

The blind spot is that most people exert influence the wrong way. They tend to influence others as they like to be influenced, and that is completely wrong. You need to adapt your approach to the person and to the situation. As you master charisma, you must influence others in the way they want. Just because you are getting short-term compliance does not mean you have influence over others. Charismatic people don't seek short-term compliance; they are after long-term influence. Short-term is easier, but it works only when you are around, as opposed to long-term influence, which works no matter where you are.

APPLICATION

When people attempt to persuade and influence, they tend to use techniques that are old-school and that no longer work. Make sure you remove these common blunders from your persuasion and influence techniques:

- Getting too friendly too fast
- The data dump—too much information
- Persuading people in the way you like to be persuaded
- Using force or coercion
- Tired old-school closing tactics
- Winning the argument but losing the ability to influence
- Changing your demeanor when you attempt to influence

EXAMPLE

Winston Churchill is considered one of the most influential speakers in modern history. He was known as a fearless and inspirational leader in the United Kingdom and led the British people through many challenges during World War II. He would spellbind audiences as he spoke. Some claimed to leave lightheaded after hearing one of his dynamic presentations. He was persuasive, had an incredible imagination, and was able to inspire the troops. His ability to use his voice was one of the elements that engaged the audience and allowed him to influence others to see his point of view. He would start with a slow pace, connect with the audience, and then increase his rate of speech to increase the energy of the room. His ability to influence increased his charisma.

CHARISMA KEY

The power of influence enables and empowers you to read people instantly, get others to take immediate action, and win over your enemies. The first key to enhance your influence is to help people influence themselves. Take some time today to be more conscious of your ability to influence. Focus on asking people more questions, reading their body language, and discovering their true needs. Try to be more aware of ways you can help them persuade themselves. When you do this, you will be able to help them influence themselves. Today, take your persuasion IQ (www.persuasioniq.com) and see where your strengths and weaknesses rank.

Rate Your Ability to Influence
Add your score to page 182.

0	1	2	3	4	5	6	7	8	9	10
Poor		*Weak*			*Average*		*Strong*			*Perfect*

CHAPTER 19

STORYTELLING:
CREATE THE IMAGE

Stories are the creative conversion of life itself into a more powerful, clearer, more meaningful experience. They are the currency of human contact.

— Robert McKee

Stories are powerful tools for developing charisma. Stories draw your audience in and help them understand and appreciate your message. When we hear a well-told story, we automatically tune in and want to know what happens next. We can all think of a time when we were in an audience and not paying attention to the speaker. We were off in our own world when, all of a sudden, we perked up and started to listen because the speaker had shifted to telling a story. Facts and figures are much more likely to strike a chord with your audience when they are coupled with relevant, powerful stories.

When you understand the essential storytelling components and how to use them, you will be able to influence and touch people's hearts with the messages you want to convey. The first and probably the most powerful element of a good story is that it should engage the emotions. When people's emotions are in play, they will be more inclined to connect with you and your message. Stories help you establish common ground, create more connectivity, and generate more attention and receptivity. Effective storytelling is the difference between communicating and convincing, between presenting and persuading, between lecturing and touching hearts.

A big part of whether or not your message is influential is whether or not the audience can believe in you. Use stories to build rapport with your audience. When you don't have an opportunity to build rapport and trust with every individual in your audience on a one-on-one basis, stories can answer their questions about who you are, what you represent, and what you want from them. If you don't answer these questions for them, they will draw their own conclusions. Why take the chance that they might draw the wrong conclusions? Do you want them to view you as funny, honest, or down-to-earth? Identify the main points you want to get across, and select your stories accordingly. Hearing your story might be as close as they will ever get to having a firsthand experience with you.

Meaningful stories inspire listeners to reach the same conclusion you have reached. People value their own conclusions more highly than yours; so if you can make your story their story, you will be much more influential. Human beings are drawn to anything that gives them "answers." Use stories to help your audience answer some of their own questions. When you are successful in doing this, your message will grow and develop in your audience's minds and hearts. They might not remember much about your presentation, but a good story and its underlying message will get played over and over again in your listeners' minds.

Positively engaging the audience's emotions with a story is one way to make a point that might otherwise meet with resistance to you or your message. Stories are less prone to make others feel defensive or feel as though you are critiquing or making demands of them. Instead of bluntly presenting your objections or differing opinions, bypass their resistance by presenting your point of view in a nonthreatening and even entertaining way. Often people staunchly defend their positions not because they are so committed to them, but because they simply must protect their need to be right and avoid the embarrassment of being wrong. If you can keep from triggering this emotional defense mechanism, you will be amazed at how much more open your audience will be to considering your ideas.

BLIND SPOT

How hard can telling a story be? You probably hear and tell stories all the time. Like most people, you probably think you're okay in this category, but others may say you are dull, boring—that your stories go on too long or are way too complicated. Charismatic people, however, can tell vivid, spellbinding stories that captivate and influence others without being obvious. Their stories come alive and create an atmosphere that helps others want to be influenced by them. Every eye in the room is focused on them and paying attention to their story; the audience never loses interest. Can you really tell an engaging, influential story?

APPLICATION

What is it that will make your story come alive? What can you do to make your audience sit on the edge of their chairs and follow your every word? How can you master the art of storytelling? Here are a few suggestions:

- Keep the story simple—no more than three or four points.
- Be animated and full of energy.
- Get your body and voice involved as part of the story.
- Get the audience to participate both physically and mentally.
- Always practice your stories on a third party.
- Speak clearly and articulate every word.
- Involve emotions for a lasting impact.

EXAMPLE

When I think of someone who could tell an engaging story, I think of Mark Twain. He was born in 1835 and became a prolific author. Some of his famous writings are *The Adventures of Tom Sawyer, The Prince and the Pauper, Adventures of Huckleberry Finn,* and *A Connecticut Yankee in King Arthur's Court.* He had the ability to make a story come alive not only on paper, but also in person. His ability to write and tell stories enabled him to become friends with presidents, town locals, industrialists, and royalty. He was a sought-after speaker and could get any audience to sit on the edge of their seats. Mark Twain will always be remembered for his ability to capture an audience with his stories.

CHARISMA KEY

Practice telling a story to everyone you meet today. It could be a simple story about where you ate lunch. Get their mouths to water as you describe the food. Get them to laugh as you recount how you had an embarrassing moment. This is how you will fine-tune your storytelling skills. Try to make your experience their experience. Learn to paint the picture for them. As you grow in your ability to tell stories, you can learn to create the right setting. You can involve the sights, the sounds, the smells, the feelings; the more you add to your story, the more you will draw your audience in. You want your audience to see your story in their minds' eyes, playing it out like a movie. You want them to take the story home, to have a place in their hearts for years to come.

Rate Your Ability to Tell Stories
Add your score to page 182.

0	1	2	3	4	5	6	7	8	9	10
Poor		*Weak*			*Average*		*Strong*			*Perfect*

CHAPTER 20

EYE CONTACT:
CONVERSING WITHOUT SPEAKING

An eye can threaten like a loaded and leveled gun, or it can
insult like hissing or kicking; or, in its altered mood, by beams
of kindness, it can make the heart dance for joy.

— RALPH WALDO EMERSON

Through the eyes, the audience can gauge the truthfulness, intelligence, and feelings of a speaker. Not making eye contact when we
ought to can have devastating results. Charisma is enhanced with
perfect, engaging eye contact. Do you have the eyes of a magnetic
person? Do your eyes attract and mesmerize others?

Charismatic people have the ability to engage others in eye contact and create an instant connection. The longer you hold a mutual
gaze with someone, the more you are rated as having high self-
esteem. However, it is critical that you do not stare at the person
100 percent of the time. You need to be able to gauge how much

eye contact someone can handle. Besides, looking at someone 100 percent of the time means one of two things: You are either very angry, or you are falling in love.

Learn to mirror their eye contact. If someone isn't able to maintain eye contact with you, then you need to decrease your eye contact to maintain the connectivity. As a general rule (one that gets adjusted slightly for each person), maintaining eye contact 70 percent of the time will work with most people. When people are uncomfortable around you, have low self-esteem, or are unsure about themselves or the situation, they will find it hard to maintain eye contact. This feeling can also be heightened if they feel threatened or if you are perceived as an authority figure.

We know people want to feel special and have their egos enhanced. When you can look them in the eye, they tend to feel that you care or that you are speaking directly to them. With eye contact, you can help them feel important and they will become the focal point during the conversation. When you break eye contact too often or too soon, you can also break the connection. In a group situation, gaze at each section of the room. Even though you are not looking at each person individually, you appear to be. Your eyes can speak louder than your voice. As Ralph Waldo Emerson said, "The eyes of men converse as much as their tongues."

The pupils of our eyes are among the most sensitive and complicated parts of our body. They will dilate when someone is aroused or interested, and this dilation is the result of years of evolution. It is an automatic eye function that allows more light into your eyes in order to catch additional information. Being able to see each other's eyes is so important to our communication and trust levels that we usually distrust a person wearing sunglasses. We assume that the use of sunglasses is a direct attempt to hide the eyes for fear that the eyes will reveal the true message.

We judge each other not only by the length of eye contact, but by the eyes themselves. Bloodshot eyes are less credible (and harder to look at) than normal-looking eyes. Larger pupils are rated as being more attractive. Take a look at some magazine covers. The pupils of the models are touched up to make them bigger and more attractive, probably because, when we become excited or happy, our pupils tend to dilate. Photos of people with enlarged pupils are subconsciously rated as more attractive.

BLIND SPOT

The blind spot is thinking, "How hard can this be?" But mastering eye contact takes some practice. A typical mistake is the length of our eye contact. One size does not fit all. One standard gaze will not connect with everyone, but you have to vary your eye contact depending on the person, culture, personality, and even race. Most people tend to stare others down even though they don't intend to. Having influence and charisma is difficult when you make people feel uncomfortable. We've all been told to make eye contact but were never told with whom, when, why, or even for how long. Many people get tense with the length of your eye contact.

APPLICATION

How can you enhance your ability to improve your eye contact and learn to connect with others? You can use eye contact to assess whether you have developed rapport with someone. Here are some pointers to improve your eye contact and rapport.

- Switch the eye you are looking at. If the other person does the same, then you have developed rapport.

- When eye contact has been made, start nodding in the yes motion. If the listener does the same, then you have developed rapport.

- Once you have established good eye contact for three to five seconds, look away. If they do the same, then you have developed rapport.

- Increase your gaze time and see if their pupils dilate. If they look away, then you have *not* developed rapport.

- When you have established eye contact and it seems like no one is home, you have *not* developed rapport.

- When you make eye contact and smile, and they don't smile back, you have *not* developed rapport.

EXAMPLE

An excellent presidential example (regardless of political affiliation) is President Bill Clinton. He had many of the pieces of the charisma puzzle, especially eye contact. Those who have met Bill Clinton say he is inspiring and genuinely interested in the people in his presence. When he talks to you, his eyes are also talking. His eyes treat you like the most important person on Earth. His gaze makes you feel in awe and comfortable at the same time. You feel as though he cares and what you are saying is important. His chief of staff Leon Panetta reiterates how Bill Clinton could make anyone feel at home and feel like the only person in the room with him.

CHARISMA KEY

Apply your ability to make great eye contact. It sounds easy on paper, but it is all about application. When you feel anxious, dominated, or nervous, you will find it hard to maintain eye contact. Take a deep breath and realize what you are doing. Get control of your emotions, and make a mental note that the other person is just as human as you are. If you are still having challenges, just look at the bridge of the person's nose. This will settle your nerves, and the other individual will have no idea you are looking there. You can also switch between eyes or between eyes and the mouth. Make sure you are not staring them down. Today, practice using the right amount of eye contact to connect and build rapport.

Rate Your Eye Contact
Add your score to page 182.

0	1	2	3	4	5	6	7	8	9	10
Poor		*Weak*			*Average*		*Strong*			*Perfect*

CHAPTER 21

LISTENING:
SAY WHAT?

Make a habit of dominating the listening and let the customer
dominate the talking.

— BRIAN TRACY

Listening and understanding enhance charisma. Everything you need to know to help, change, or influence someone can be discovered by truly listening. You will be able to inspire, motivate, and gain trust by learning to listen. People feel more respected and valued when you listen to what they have say. Listening enables you to solve problems faster and it increases their trust in you. The bottom line is that it also reduces miscommunication, overall mistakes, and misunderstandings. Listening is a simple thing to do, and all it costs you is a small investment of your time.

Good listening is *not* nodding your head and pretending to care. Good listening is *not* looking people in the eye while you mentally prepare what to say next. You have to acknowledge what is being said and let the other person know that you understand. Listen with your eyes, and read the speaker's nonverbal behavior. Listen with your ears to the words, to the rate of speech, and to the tone of voice. Listen with your heart to find out what the person is really trying to say. Great listening is all about helping people feel good about themselves and about you. This type of listening is also about demonstrating that you care.

Listening connects you with people and establishes rapport. We love to talk about ourselves; that is Influence 101. When you become a great listener, people will tell you everything you need to know to influence them. All of us can become better listeners, and the returns on listening are incredible. Most complaints about the influence process involve the feeling that the person talked too much and did not listen to what the other person really needed. We are so determined to churn out all the reasons they should do business with us or like our idea that we forget they have their own needs and wants. We think we're being helpful by offering lengthy, in-depth explanations. Let's face it: We're self-centered, self-interested, and self-absorbed, and we always focus on ourselves. So we talk too much because we like to feel important, knowledgeable, and helpful.

Mastering the art of listening will enable you to get others more involved in your message and make them feel more understood. Listening increases your comprehension, and lets you control the conversation. Dale Carnegie asserted many years ago that listening is one of the most crucial human relations skills that we all should work on. Listening is how we find out people's preferences, desires, wants, and needs. It is how we learn to customize our message to them. Of all the skills you can master, listening is probably the one that will pay off the most. We think we understand people's wants and needs, but we don't really until we can sincerely and accurately listen.

BLIND SPOT

The blind spot in listening is a huge denial factor. Most people say there is no problem—"I can listen!" We all have ears and think we can listen, but the truth is that we are only hearing. Many large corporations have instituted listening training (calling it by various names), but most people think it is a waste of time. Most of the challenges in our relationships, businesses, and even world affairs could be resolved if two people could sit down and truly listen to each other. All it takes is a little mental exertion and listening with your ears, your eyes, and your heart. When you are perceived as a poor listener, you are judged as self-centered, disinterested, and uncharismatic.

APPLICATION

With enhanced listening skills, you will know what others are thinking and feeling and how to influence them. Do you want to know the secret of the masters? Here are guidelines you can use to increase your listening skills and influence with people:

- Give them your undivided attention, and keep distractions to a minimum.
- Lean forward and look them directly in their face.
- Pretend you have all the time in the world.
- Nod your head and agree with verbal sounds like "uh-huh."
- Never interrupt; keep the conversation going with questions.
- Pause before replying.

Example

Larry King is a great listener. He started doing radio interviews in Florida in the 1950s and began the *Larry King Live* show on CNN in 1985. He has been recognized as one of the premier broadcasters of all time, winning numerous awards. He has made a career out of listening by interviewing more than 40,000 people on his shows. King has said, "I remind myself every morning: Nothing I say this day will teach me anything. So if I'm going to learn, I must do it by listening." Interviewers like Larry King are able to get people to open up and bare their souls. Watch them, observe their listening skills, and learn how they use simple questions to get people to tell everything the interviewer is looking for.

CHARISMA KEY

Today, let's focus on really listening. Understand that real listening takes some mental exertion and concentration. Try letting others talk without interruption. Don't attempt to finish their sentences or jump into what they are saying just to get your point across and enhance your ego. When they finish, ask another question to keep them talking. This technique helps you gauge your understanding of what they really need or want. Read their nonverbal behavior and try to sense how you would feel if you were the other person. The big blunder is prejudging or categorizing others before or during a conversation. When you prejudge someone, it only sucks the life out of you, out of the conversation, and out of how they feel about you. When you don't give it your best effort, it is obvious to the person.

Rate Your Listening
Add your score to page 182.

0	1	2	3	4	5	6	7	8	9	10
Poor		*Weak*			*Average*		*Strong*		*Perfect*	

CHAPTER 22

RAPPORT:
THE INSTANT CONNECTION

It is not your customer's job to remember you. It is your
obligation and responsibility to make sure they don't have the
chance to forget you.

—**Patricia Fripp**

We have all met someone who, after just a few seconds of being
together, we felt an instant connection or bond with them. We also
have probably all met someone whom we instantly did not like and
did not want to be around. When you can develop rapport, when
you can connect with anyone, when others feel comfortable around
you, then you can enhance the effect of your charisma. Others will
pay more attention to you, they will want to be influenced by you,
and they will open up more readily. Rapport is when two (or more)
people synchronize mentally, physically, and vocally. If you discon-

nect, it will take an hour or more to repair the connection. How do you come across to others? Can you instantly develop a rapport with someone? This is a vital skill of charismatic people: to instantly connect with someone without even thinking about it.

Rapport creates trust and puts us on the same wavelength as the other person or audience. You probably have seen rapport at work many times. Remember when you met a perfect stranger and just hit it off? Finding plenty to talk about, you almost felt as if you had met before. The connection just felt right. You became so comfortable that you could talk about practically anything, and you lost track of time. You developed such a strong bond with the person that you knew what she was going to say. Everything just clicked between the two of you, and you felt very close to this person. You felt your ideas were in sync, and you enjoyed your time together. This is rapport.

You can speed up the natural process of connecting and building rapport by understanding the unspoken message. How do you make sure you are really developing rapport? You want to be friendly, but not fake. You want to be engaging, but not annoying. You need to develop a natural instinct for building rapport. You need to know whether you are building rapport and, if not, how to adjust your conversation. To do this, you have to be able to read nonverbal cues, detect unspoken messages, and decipher the true feelings behind facial expressions, body language, and attitude.

With rapport, people want to be around you, like to be around you, and feel better about themselves for being around you. Thus the power of your charisma grows. One challenge that people face when building rapport and charisma is that they can lose that connection just after they start to gain it. What do I mean? Most people don't know how to maintain rapport throughout the entire exchange. They know how to break the ice and get people to open up. Then, when they get around to asking someone to help, to donate money, or to change their lives, something strange happens. All of a sudden, they get serious and their demeanor changes. What is the other person going to think? Someone they were joking with for the past ten minutes has now completely morphed into a different person. Which one is real? This abrupt change in persona breaks rapport and seems incongruent to others.

BLIND SPOT

We are so concerned about how we look, what is happening in our lives, what we have to do next, and how to boost our own self-esteem that we forget to connect and build rapport with others. We need to be aware of two blind spots. The first is not taking the time to really care about and connect with other people. The second is when we make weak, fake, and insincere efforts to connect, our efforts actually come across that way. The other person won't tell you, so you think you're connecting. Rapport is critical to charisma, and, even if people talk to you or are nice to you, you are not necessarily developing rapport with them.

APPLICATION

A handshake can make or break that first impression. Thus it can help or hurt rapport. Your handshake communicates strength, weakness, indifference, or even warmth. What factors are you being judged on? Here are some things you need to be aware of when you shake hands with someone:

- Length of eye contact
- Strength or weakness of grip
- Duration of handshake
- Moisture of hands
- Depth of the interlock

EXAMPLE

Whom do we all know who can develop instant rapport with one person or with millions at the same time? You have heard the name: Oprah Winfrey. She started on television in 1983 in Chicago. She quickly went from last place in the ratings to the first-place spot. Her guests and her audience feel at ease with her personality, her conversational styles, and her sincere and genuine interest in people. She uses herself and her personal life on a level that builds rapport with her fans. She is often seen crying with her guests and relating to them because she has experienced many of the same challenges in her life. She is like a good member of the family sitting down to have a chat or just to talk about your problems. She radiates empathy, uses humor, and we know she cares. Oprah *is* rapport.

CHARISMA KEY

One way to speed up your connection or rapport with people is to mirror and match. Today, try this with everyone you meet and communicate with. Without even realizing it, we often unconsciously mirror others' behavior, mannerisms, mood, and gestures. This behavior is just a natural process when we connect with someone. Have you ever noticed at social gatherings how people tend to match each other in their body language and their attitudes? When you can develop a similar demeanor with your audience, they will feel a connection with you. Remember, people are inclined to follow those they perceive as similar to themselves. If they shift in their posture, you eventually do so too. If they cross their legs, you cross your legs as well. If they smile, you smile too. Try the mirror-and-match technique today. You will be amazed how well it works.

Rate Your Ability to Gain Rapport
Add your score to page 182.

0	1	2	3	4	5	6	7	8	9	10
Poor		*Weak*			*Average*		*Strong*			*Perfect*

ADDITIONAL DELIVERY AND COMMUNICATION RESOURCES (LAWSOFCHARISMA.COM)

- Support articles
- Section support audio: "How to Win Over an Audience Every Time"
- Section worksheet

SECTION FOUR

EMPOWERING OTHERS:
CONTAGIOUS COOPERATION

FABLE: THE LION AND THE MOUSE

The king of the jungle was an enormous lion who loved his power and prestige. One day, while the lion was taking a nap, a mouse walked across his back and down his leg. Outraged, he awoke and placed his large paw on the mouse.

"Who is this little mouse?" he thought. "Doesn't he know how powerful I am and that I could squash him or eat him at anytime?" To teach the mouse a lesson, the lion began to swallow him whole.

"Pardon me, king," said the mouse. "Please forgive me this one time. I will never do it again. Please let me go, and someday I will repay the favor." The lion was amused that this little mouse thought he could ever repay the great and powerful king of the jungle. He was so tickled by the thought that he let the mouse go.

Six months later the king of the jungle got caught in the trap of a famous hunter. The hunter tied the lion up with ropes that were too thick and powerful for him to escape. The lion couldn't get loose no matter how hard he struggled; so he gave up because the situation seemed hopeless. That night the mouse was passing by and saw the lion in this predicament. While the hunter slept, the little mouse gnawed at the ropes that held the lion captive. With only one hour left until daylight, the mouse was able to free the mighty lion. As the lion escaped, the mouse smiled and said, "I told you I could repay your favor."

MEANING

Everybody you meet and everybody you know can help you achieve success and happiness. Empower others, treat others with respect, and there often will come a time when they can repay you tenfold. Learn to keep others inspired, discover how to motivate, build a united vision, and you will always have people around to help you when you need it the most.

EMPOWERING OTHERS SKILLS/TRAITS

- Inspiration
- Esteem
- Credibility
- Motivation
- Goodwill
- Vision
- Empathy
- Respect

CHAPTER 23

INSPIRATION:
STRENGTHEN AND ENERGIZE

People are not lazy. They simply have impotent goals—that is, goals that do not inspire them.

—ANTHONY ROBBINS

If you are uninspired, you will not be inspiring. Charismatic people have the ability to inspire others, to instantly lift their moods, to adjust their emotions, and to increase the energy in the room. When you see a charismatic person who inspires others to new heights, the effect looks very simple, but being charismatic and inspirational is a full-time job. It is not something you do only every once in awhile. When you have the ability to inspire others, people rise to your expectations. They want to grow and improve themselves; they thrive on your high expectations. They expect you to lift their spirits and inspire them to new heights. It is refreshing for them to feel hope, energy, and inspiration.

Unfortunately, most people already have plenty of people around them who de-inspire or disempower them. What is the opposite of hope? It is despair, which comes when we feel powerless to change events or when we lose our sense of purpose in life. Despair is a source of disorientation so profound that we can lose contact with reality. Most people don't know they are negative or stuck in despair, but they are draining the life out of everyone around them. Anybody can drive another person to do something through desperation, fear, or worry. The problem is that desperation is temporary. People who are driven by desperation or fear are typically so preoccupied with what they're trying to get away from that they can't think of anything else, let alone their own future.

The difference between using desperation instead of inspiration is that desperation promotes fear and competition, whereas inspiration promotes hope and teamwork. Desperation is usually rooted in fear. People will not appreciate feeling pressured or bullied into doing what you want them to do. They will resent you, harbor negative feelings toward you, and never want to work with you again. Desperation leads to poor decisions, forces unwanted choices, reduces options, and spawns regret. Despair is very destructive and sucks the life and energy out of people. Your goal is to inspire hope.

Samuel Smiles wrote:

> Hope is like the sun, which, as we journey towards it, casts the shadow of our burden behind us. . . . Hope tempers our troubles to our growth and our strength. It befriends us in dark hours, excites us in bright ones. It lends promise to the future and purpose to the past. It turns discouragement to determination.

If you want your charisma to last, you need to rely on the inspiration that is rooted in your emotions and your vision. The positive results that come from using inspiration are obvious. Inspired people don't need a carrot dangling in front of them to get something accomplished. You don't need to use fear tactics. When you use inspiration, people become more self-motivated and don't wait for external factors to drive them one way or the other. Getting others inspired is the only way to maintain long-term motivation. When you radiate inspiration, you move people away from despair, inaction, and blame. You give them hope in themselves and in the future. You will be able to lead and inspire with charisma and the future in mind.

BLIND SPOT

The blind spot is our own knee-jerk reaction and our standard programming to use fear and desperation when we are trying to get others to do things. That kind of tactic works in the short term, but it does not set the standard for long-term inspiration and powerful charisma. Fear is very easy to use, does not take much talent, and requires little skill. Others have used it on us, and so we are going to use it too. When we can use fear or desperation to get others to do what we want them to do, we feel empowered. We create short-term compliance, but produce long-term resentment. You probably don't even realize that fear and desperation is your automatic response when your first attempt at influence does not work.

APPLICATION

So how do you know whether you inspire others? How do you know whether you can promote teamwork? How do you know whether you are getting the best out of people? Here are a few questions to think about in order to understand whether people are inspired or stuck in desperation:

- Do others feel better about themselves after interacting with you? If so, they are inspired.
  - Do they feel worse? If so, they feel desperation.
- Do they know you are pleased or grateful for their work? If so, they are inspired.
  - Do you think you don't care? If so, they feel desperation.
- Do they know you truly care and would go to bat for them? If so, they are inspired.
  - Do they feel they are just another member of the team? If so, they feel desperation.

- Do you listen and care about their suggestions and their feedback? If so, they are inspired.
  - Do they get defensive when you critique them? If so, they feel desperation.

- Do they actively participate in meetings and conversations? If so, they are inspired.
  - Do they show little participation and are they afraid to open their mouths? If so, they feel desperation.

- Do they freely own up to their mistakes or shortcomings? If so, they are inspired.
  - Do they blame others or make it your fault? If so, they feel desperation.

EXAMPLE

George Washington was a person who inspired those around him. He was the first president of the United States of America and, before that, the commander of the Continental Army during the Revolutionary War. He was known for his unyielding character and powerful charisma. As you know from the history books, the frigid winter of 1777–1778 at Valley Forge was a time of little hope, and many were filled with despair. Washington and his army were camped out for six months, and 25 percent of his men died because of disease and exposure to the elements. Anyone else probably would have lost the dedication and the support of their troops. However, Washington was always able to inspire hope in his men and in the nation that he helped to build. During a time of great despair and little hope, he was able to inspire others to action.

CHARISMA KEY

As you develop charisma, you must inspire others to achieve new levels of success. Too many people are stuck in despair and full of hopelessness. They are in desperation because they are moving away from something. You can give them hope in their future by focusing on inspiration and by getting them moving toward something meaningful. What can you do today to help someone move from desperation to inspiration? They want to strive for something meaningful. They may have tried to do so in the past and failed. What can you do to inspire hope and help others feel they are capable of doing what you are asking them to do?

Rate Your Ability to Inspire
Add your score to page 182.

0	1	2	3	4	5	6	7	8	9	10
Poor		Weak			Average			Strong		Perfect

CHAPTER 24

ESTEEM:
UNDERSTAND THE EGO

It is amazing what you can accomplish if you do not care who
gets the credit.

— Harry S. Truman

Understanding ego is pretty simple when you think about it: We
like people who like us, and we don't like people who don't like us.
Most of us find it challenging to give praise, to boost others' self-
esteems, and to point out the positive. Heightened self-esteem is
the elusive and almost intangible aspiration of most people. It is
self-satisfaction in yourself or how much you like yourself. The key
is to understand that, to become more charismatic, you need a
healthy self-esteem and the ability to raise somebody else's self-
esteem.

We all suffer from different aspects of low self-esteem. Rather
than blame anybody or anything for the shortcoming, let's just own

up to it. People who possess a high self-esteem are strong and se-cure; they can admit when they are wrong. They are not unraveled by criticism or negativity. Their healthy self-esteem permeates every aspect of their lives: their jobs, their relationships, and their social interactions.

Understanding the basic human need for esteem is critical. When people feel wanted and important, they become much easier to influence. You would never think about physically harming others or depriving them of food and water. Yet often without even thinking about it, we hurt people emotionally or deprive them of praise or gratitude. We all want to feel accepted or to be a part of the group. We all want to be noticed and appreciated and to feel that our contributions help the cause. Not everyone wants to be recognized the same way, but everyone needs recognition. When others get that unconditional acceptance, with no strings attached, you will see their doubt and fears go out the window and feel your charisma soar.

One easy way to boost people's esteem is to offer sincere, genu-ine thanks. Show gratitude for what they have done or will do. Never assume that they know how much you care or appreciate them. For example, you see dissatisfaction in the workplace mainly because people are never thanked or given recognition for their efforts. At first it might seem a bit unnatural for you to use thanks and gratitude because most of us have not experienced an environ-ment where doing so was common, but saying thank-you is worth the energy and effort.

Also important is being able to read people and understand the signals of low self-esteem, which might be the opposite of what you think. The signs could be bullying, always having to be right, gossiping, quick to take offense, or resentment of others. Charis-matic people have the ability to read these signs in others and en-hance their self-esteem, playing on the link between esteem and performance. Boosting others' esteem increases their confidence; people have better attitudes and perform better.

All this is not to say you can never say anything negative or critical. Just be aware that one negative comment has more emo-tional impact than ten positive ones. Keep in mind that the use of praise affects us to the very core. Use it properly.

BLIND SPOT

The reality is that we all suffer low self-esteem in some aspect of our lives. Self-esteem is at an all-time low. This is a researched fact. Overall self-esteem gets lower every year, and we don't realize that many of our challenges with our daily interactions come from our low self-esteem, that is, not understanding the human ego. The blind spot is thinking we can boost someone's self-esteem by saying a few nice words. This type of praise usually comes across as insincere. Once others sense you will gain something from the exchange, your words will backfire on you every time. The need is to understand how your own low self-esteem affects your ability to radiate charisma. The second is improving your ability to realistically and sincerely boost someone else's ego.

APPLICATION

Praise costs nothing, but yields incredible results. When praise does not work, one of the reasons is that no one has ever taught you the right way to give it. For praise to work and enhance your charisma, certain elements must be included.

- Be specific.
- Praise something the person can't refute.
- Be sincere with your words.
- Public praise is more powerful than private praise.
- Be prompt with your praise.
- Keep all praise positive.

EXAMPLE

When we show people that they are important, we increase our charisma and our influence with them. Andrew Carnegie was a successful businessman and philanthropist. He was an immigrant to the United States and started in the railroad business as a telegrapher, which eventually led to investments in railroads and steel. In terms of real dollars, he is often regarded as the second wealthiest man in history after John D. Rockefeller. Andrew Carnegie devised a plan to sell his steel to the Pennsylvania Railroad. When he built a new steel mill in Pittsburgh, he named it the J. Edgar Thompson Steel Works, after the president of the Pennsylvania Railroad. Thompson was so flattered by the honor that he purchased steel exclusively from Carnegie. Understanding esteem is so simple, yet so powerful.

CHARISMA KEY

Many don't give praise because they are concerned that it will appear phony, that people won't believe it, or that others might even get upset. The way I see it, if you have any of these concerns, you probably aren't phony. When you truly care about others and are specific in your praise, your words will open doors and increase your charisma. Spend some time today praising little things, and then it will be much easier in the long run to praise the bigger things. Look for people to praise. You'll be surprised how often you can praise, how easy it will become to praise, and how well praise works. Being aware that most of us don't praise because of our own lack of esteem will put praise into perspective and help us be more aware of the praise we give out. Remember, praise is free.

Rate Your Ability to Raise Esteem
Add your score to page 182.

0	1	2	3	4	5	6	7	8	9	10
Poor		*Weak*			*Average*		*Strong*			*Perfect*

CHAPTER 25

CREDIBILITY:
REALITY VERSUS PERCEPTION

One can stand as the greatest orator the world has known,
possess the quickest mind, employ the cleverest psychology
and have mastered all the technical devices of argument, but
if one is not credible one might just as well preach to the
pelicans.

—GERRY SPENCE

When you have credibility, people see you as believable, and you
come across having the expertise to make things happen or solve
their challenges. Credibility is based on three things: your knowledge, your track record, and your appearance. What has happened
in the past? Have you kept all your promises? Are you known for
revealing half-truths or, even worse, hiding some of the truth? Do
you keep all of your commitments? Do you own up to your mis-

takes? Do you face reality with confidence? The answers to all these questions will help or hurt your perception of credibility.

Credibility increases when you leave no gap between what you say and what you do. The perception is that you are willing and able to do what you say you can do. High credibility enhances the trust of others and increases their commitment. Low credibility diminishes motivation, breeds criticism, and reveals itself in the form of a lack of support. When you reach full charisma, you are a role model. You are doing what you are asking others to do. You are on the front line, with your sleeves rolled up, doing what needs to be done. You are noticeable, and you practice what you preach.

Whether it is fair or not, how you present yourself and your demeanor can either help or hurt your perception of credibility. Learn to present yourself in a calm, prepared, and authoritative manner. By getting overly emotional or flustered, you will only throw your credibility out the window. Credible people do not run around like headless chickens. They are not disorganized or look as though they're out of control. Credible people are in control and composed at all times. Even if they don't feel that way on the inside, they look that way on the outside. Studies show that showing up on time and being organized dramatically enhances the initial perception of credibility.

Two things that dramatically hurt credibility are the appearance of deception and coming across as too good to be true.

- *Deception:* Any type of lying or deception is usually obvious to others, and its effect on credibility is immediate. Many people think that, if they are not called on a lie, they got away with it. Not true. Others will subconsciously sense the lie and make a mental note without saying anything. You should never risk blowing your credibility with any form of deception. Deception just is not worth it, and the chances are high that you are *not* going to get away with it.

- *Being Too Good to Be True:* To offset the effect of this, reveal a weakness. Interestingly, people are so skeptical these days that they are looking for some type of weakness in you or your product. If you don't show them a weakness, preferably a minor one, they will assign one to you. For example, if your product or service is the most expensive, don't hide that weakness. Reveal it as a strength: "It is top of the line, has more features, and lasts twice as long as the other leading brand." Revealing a small weakness tends to make people view you as more honest and credible than those who try to cover up faults and shortcomings. Our credibility increases when we are big enough to own up to our mistakes and weaknesses. People can forgive weakness, but they won't be as quick to forgive coverups.

BLIND SPOT

Credibility is essential to charisma. The blind spot with credibility is assuming that you have it and that you are believable. You could be the smartest person in your field or even the most qualified, but if that is not the perception, you have no credibility. You could even be an expert, but if you don't always come across that way, you are not credible. If somebody reveals something negative about you or your company, your credibility is shot. We don't often think about credibility because we believe ourselves to be credible. We always tell the truth, and we know that we have the expertise. This might be true, but credibility is a perception, not a fact. It is not given; it is earned.

APPLICATION

As you know, lying and deception destroy any credibility you might have earned in the past. Most people won't call you a liar to your face, but they will quietly decide not to believe anything you say. The person will make up an excuse ("I need more information," "Talk to me later," "I'll think about it"), and you will never hear from them again. What red flags should you be watching for? How do you know if you suffer from low credibility? Do any of the following things happen to you?

- Complaints to your superiors
- Needing references
- Not returning calls

- Canceling appointments
- Failing to give you repeat business
- Exhibiting no loyalty

EXAMPLE

Warren Buffett, born in 1930 in Omaha, Nebraska, is one of the most successful investors in history and one of the richest men in the world. He is also known for being very frugal and has pledged to give away 85 percent of his wealth. He was voted the top money manager of the twentieth century. If you want to know about the financial sector, if you want to know which stocks to invest in, talk to Warren Buffett. If you want to know anything about money, talk to Warren Buffett. He has the experience, the track record, and the credibility to make everyone want to listen. Even when you watch him speak, his mannerisms and demeanor don't turn you off, but only increase his credibility. He mentored with the best (Benjamin Graham), he trained with the best (Dale Carnegie course), and his track record is the best (most successful investor of all time).

CHARISMA KEY

The key is to continually enhance your credibility (no matter where you are starting). What can you do to overcome credibility challenges? Be overprepared and anticipate any question you might face. You can't have credibility or charisma if you are winging it. Today, find ways to increase your credibility with people without coming across as a braggart. What can you do or say to reveal your expertise, qualifications, education, or experience so that you will be perceived as the expert? Get creative; for example, have someone with credibility introduce you.

Rate Your Credibility
Add your score to page 182.

0	1	2	3	4	5	6	7	8	9	10
Poor		*Weak*			*Average*		*Strong*			*Perfect*

CHAPTER 26

MOTIVATION:
LIGHT THEIR FIRE

Motivation is the art of getting people to do what you want
them to do because they want to do it.

— DWIGHT D. EISENHOWER

How do you turn people's basic wants and needs into motivation?
How do you get them to do what they need to do even though they
don't feel like doing it or want to do it? Charismatic people get
others to motivate themselves for the long term. They are able to
help others visualize goals and make them feel they can attain those
goals. Such motivation also allows them to set their own goals,
solve their own challenges, make their own decisions, but still feel
they are on the team. The journey to achieve goals can get long,
hard, tiring, and frustrating. Your charisma is what carries them,
motivates them, and lifts their spirits when they are feeling down.
What if they do get down? It will happen: Feeling low at times is

inevitable. Telling others they will never feel down or unmotivated will backfire on you. Prepare their minds for the times when things get hard or when success seems improbable.

You can enhance motivation and empower people in two ways. The first is personal development. When you help others use their minds, increase their knowledge, and enhance their skills, you will find untapped drive and motivation. They will develop a sense of urgency and direction that will propel them faster and higher than before. We know when you help others learn and grow, they become more optimistic and motivated. Their self-esteem increases. They feel they have the tools and mental capital they need to be successful. The focus on personal development will get them to use their minds, their knowledge, and their skills. Charismatic people help others develop a hunger for knowledge and feel an inner need to improve themselves. Charismatic people help others want to grow, improve, and accomplish things they were not able to do in the past, things that stretch and challenge them. When people's capacity and desire for growth increases, motivation becomes easy.

The second way to motivate and empower others is to get them to set goals. We live in a world where we want everything now. We want a quick fix. We want instant gratification and immediate results. Moreover, we want it all with minimal effort. How do you motivate this type of person? One way is to understand the power of goal setting, a concept that has been abused because it has been used the wrong way. Very few really know how to do it. The key is not only helping others to set and achieve goals, but also being able to communicate exactly what each goal is. People should welcome the new challenge and believe they can meet it. They also should know you are committed to them and believe they can achieve their goal.

On the surface, most people will resist goal setting because they never had anyone teach them the right way to do it. However, human beings are designed to set and achieve goals. Your job is to help them rediscover the need to set objectives and have a target in their lives. Helping others make goals changes and increases their future expectations. Charisma is about helping them discover what they want to achieve and see themselves achieving it. Helping them stretch themselves will increase their motivation and drive.

BLIND SPOT

Our blind spot is thinking that what motivates us will motivate others. Face it: We are all different, have different personalities, and are motivated by different things. In fact, one type of motivation that worked for someone today could be useless tomorrow. Did you know that most managers rank compensation as the number one reason people are motivated to go to work? But when you ask employees for the number one thing that motivates them, the response is having an interesting and an inspiring place to work. Compensation comes in at number five. Do you really know what motivates others? Learn to read others and understand what motivates them.

APPLICATION

We already know that true motivation does not involve manipulation, force, or demeaning people. In the workplace, what can we apply right now to enhance and increase employee motivation?

- Clear and concise expectations
- Increased training and personal development
- Jointly setting realistic and exciting goals
- Limiting negative reinforcement and pessimistic coworkers
- Recognizing and rewarding improvement
- Making the workplace fun, interesting, and stimulating
- Making sure workers have the tools and resources they need

EXAMPLE

One of the greatest motivators was the legendary football coach Vince Lombardi. Born in 1913, his claim to fame was five league championships while coaching the Green Bay Packers in the NFL, including winning the first two Super Bowls ever played. He knew that the way to victory was paved with a combined effort of multiple individuals. His players all agree that he motivated them to be their very best. His players said he would stay up until 3 A.M. devising plays to beat the competition. He drove his players to excellence. Even though he was quick to yell, he used kind words and positive emotions when he needed them. One thing many of his players echoed was, "We would go through fire for him."

CHARISMA KEY

Strive to remember that with charisma you become a motivating force for others. Many of those you will attempt to motivate have tried to do what you are asking them to do, but could not. Human beings are notorious for trying something once or twice and, if they are not successful, assuming that they will always fail in that particular activity. This tendency decreases their ability to want to learn and lowers their expectation of potential success. Help them dream, give them the tools to achieve success, and motivate them to make it happen. Today, find someone you can motivate by giving them higher expectations, realistic goals, and the tools to achieve them.

Rate Your Ability to Motivate
Add your score to page 182.

0	1	2	3	4	5	6	7	8	9	10
Poor		*Weak*			*Average*		*Strong*			*Perfect*

CHAPTER 27

GOODWILL:
CHARITY AND COMPASSION

I am certain that after the dust of centuries has passed over our cities, we, too, will be remembered not for victories or defeats in battle or politics, but for our contribution to the human spirit.

—JOHN F. KENNEDY

Many people think that, when they get into positions of prominence, others should be serving them or looking up to them. This is a great way to turn people off and decrease your charisma. If your only focus is on you, then eventually all the focus will be off you. Others might try to get your attention, but they are only after you for money or recognition; they are not seeking you out because of who you are. When you start to focus on others, show kindness, and offer charity and goodwill, the focus will return to you. When you look for the good in others, you become better yourself. When you start looking for ways to serve, not only do you open the doors to influence, but you also increase your well-being and your happiness.

Having goodwill entails being friendly and showing genuine concern for other people. Aristotle said, "We consider as friends those who wish good things for us and who are pained when bad things happen to us." This type of concern and kindness means being perceptive and thoughtful. It means being considerate in all your encounters. Always be polite, and show genuine concern to those around you. That concern is the foundation for all interactions and creates a mood of reciprocity and charisma. You will win hearts and loyalty through compassion and goodwill.

You demonstrate goodwill by focusing on positives and by being careful with the negatives. Don't be harsh or forceful when dealing with people. Remember, people can be highly sensitive and feel overly vulnerable. Watch your statements and your actions, and always show that you have the audience's best interest in mind. Never criticize someone unless you really need to, and then do it the right way. Criticism can damage your relationship, destroy the connection with the person, and hurt your charisma. Anytime you make someone feel stupid, you are perceived as inconsiderate and your ability to influence diminishes. Instead, find something positive and show goodwill. This will increase acceptance and self-confidence. Show that you care, show some goodwill, and you will automatically increase your charisma.

A big part of goodwill is the mindset of *abundance*, which is a state of mind that allows you to give, knowing that the universe will reward you. You don't give for the sake of reward; you give because giving is the right thing to do. As author Stephen Covey said, "The abundance mentality flows out of a deep inner sense of personal worth and security. It is the paradigm that there is plenty out there and enough to spare for everybody. . . . It opens possibilities, options, alternatives, and creativity." You know that giving of your time, money, or even skills is not only the right thing to do, it increases your abundance, your health, your happiness, and your charisma. Get past the scarcity mentality that society has given you, and see the abundance the world has to offer. Realize that we are all on the same human team and that we all have our strengths and weaknesses. Always be willing to share your strengths, and someone will come along to help you with your weaknesses.

BLIND SPOT

Having a good heart, serving others, and showing goodwill is something most of us think we are already doing. Ask yourself whether you can do more. Showing sincere kindness to others empowers them and increases your charisma. We don't develop goodwill by getting something from someone; we show goodwill because it is the right thing to do. The blind spot is thinking that, "When I arrive [whatever and whenever that may be], I will be kinder, be more charitable, and offer more goodwill. When I have more time and money, I will give back." The time to start showing more goodwill is now. The time to increase your charity is today.

APPLICATION

The application is simple. Start giving of yourself, start caring about others, and start showing your goodwill. You will be amazed at how much people will want to be around you, and you will become a happier person. Try some of these simple things to get started:

- Do something to improve someone's day.
- Offer a compliment when it is least expected.
- Sincerely ask how another person is doing.
- Look for the small opportunities to serve.
- Pay the toll of the person behind you.
- Leave a big tip.
- Give 10 percent of your income to a church, charity, or cause.

EXAMPLE

When I think of goodwill, I always think of the *Chicken Soup for the Soul* guys, Mark Victor Hansen and Jack Canfield. They created the series of books that has sold over 100 million copies around the world. One of the reasons for their success is that they are both genuinely good people. They are willing to help others, give back, and make the world a better place. You could be a stranger meeting either one of them at an airport, and they would be more than willing to help you. They also have dedicated 10 percent of the proceeds of each book to charity, and they have donated millions of dollars to charities around the world. They are big believers that the more you give, the more you get. Some would say, sure, they have the money to give, so it's no big deal. Well, when they were broke and the first book came out, they already had committed to give 10 percent of the royalties to charity. They both believe that this goodwill is a key factor in their success.

CHARISMA KEY

Be aware of the world around you. If you are like most people, you are stuck on your own life. Try to focus on everyone else you meet. Substitute positive thinking for all the negative thoughts and comments about other people. Look for the good in others, and strive to bring out the best in them. When you can improve the life of everyone you meet (it could take only seconds) in some subtle way, you will radiate goodwill. Everyone needs a little help now and then. Today, look for a chance to practice goodwill, provide a bit of service. You will see everyone benefit.

Rate Your Goodwill
Add your score to page 182.

0	1	2	3	4	5	6	7	8	9	10
Poor		*Weak*			*Average*		*Strong*			*Perfect*

CHAPTER 28

VISION:
SEE IT, TASTE IT, TOUCH IT, FEEL IT

Where there is no vision, the people perish.

— PROVERBS 29:18

Don't confuse a visionary person with one who has a vision. A visionary person tends to talk a lot without doing much. A person with vision is able to recruit others to help realize a vision. Such a person has no doubt about the vision, is always moving toward it, and possesses an inner strength that drives the person past the inevitable challenges. A charismatic person must be able to communicate the vision, get buy-in or commitment from others, and make the vision so compelling that it seems realistic. A vision inspires and empowers us to reach for the stars. It enables us to get past our fears and our worries about what could go wrong. It allows us to drop preconceived notions, move past barriers, and exceed previous limitations. When you have charisma, your vision is driven by your passion and conviction.

The vision of a charismatic person empowers others to have confidence not only in themselves, but in their personal ability to do what it takes to carry out the vision. Having vision bonds people together and creates a common purpose. The challenge, however, is that, when a vision is presented, it doesn't create ownership. If the perception of others is that the effort is all for you—all about you—and they don't know where they fit in, they can feel manipulated and will not take ownership. They want to know what is in it for them in the long term. Why should they support you and your vision? Remember, most people feel more comfortable with the status quo than they do about risking anything for a better future. A true vision not only diminishes the fear of failure and negative thinking, but also promotes synergy. Your vision creates a link from the present state to the future objective.

All human beings yearn for direction and guidance. That's why someone with a vision is so appealing and influential. Charismatic people are able to create a strong, clear vision of the future. People will jump on board when they see a vivid vision in place that they can touch, taste, feel, or see. No one wants to get on board a sinking ship. People want to be in the know. What's the plan? Where are we going? What are we aiming for? Your goal is to powerfully present how your vision is the solution to their problems. Your vision must bridge the gap between their present state and the desired situation—from where they are to where they want to be.

Vision is powerful because it keeps us focused on a future objective instead of getting stuck in day-to-day preoccupations. It gives us focus and a future direction. It creates a big picture. A cohesive common vision brings people together and unites them with common goals and objectives. Charismatic people have a clearly defined vision and are filled with great enthusiasm and expectations. More than anything else in life, vision—whether it's yours or somebody else's—dictates your daily decisions. When the vision is clear, the right decisions are easier to make.

BLIND SPOT

We have all been to those rah-rah motivational meetings where the future is laid out and everyone is supposed to get excited and jump on board. The CEO gets energized, has great enthusiasm, and proclaims to the whole room why everyone should endorse the vision. Everyone politely listens and waits for the meeting to be over; the audience might even respond with a lot of applause. The next day nothing has changed, and everything goes back to normal. The blind spot is thinking that when others pretend to be excited about your vision that it will compel them to buy into it. Even if the vision is in the best interests of others, if they don't see it and feel it, they will withhold ownership.

APPLICATION

What does it take to create a compelling, vibrant vision that excites others and causes them to want to join with you? When you create a vision, you can implement a few critical elements that cause others to commit themselves to the cause.

- Create a vision that everyone can share and that enables everyone to win.
- Paint the picture that makes the vision come alive.
- Establish a common goal or a common enemy.
- Make sure your objective is clear and precise, because unrealistic or ambiguous visions die fast.
- Be able to offer an action plan that seems realistic.

EXAMPLE

Jack Welch is a great example of a visionary charismatic person. He transformed GE with his ability to create, deliver, and inspire vision. He was known for never compromising and he meant whatever he said. In the 1980s, Welch had the vision of streamlining GE into a more competitive company. He created a vision to eliminate inefficiency and cut corporate red tape. He had everyone buy into the concept that, if any company under GE was not number one or number two in its industry, GE should sell it. Initially he had his critics, but his vision, charisma, and conviction turned his goals into reality. Welch pushed people to perform, but he also handed out great rewards. He went on to earn great respect not only from GE, but from all of corporate America.

CHARISMA KEY

The key today is to help someone get out of the worries of the past and into a vision of the future. Understand that the opposite of vision is worry. When people are stuck on worry, their vision of the future is not strong enough to overcome their worries. They can't see themselves doing what they want to do or what you've asked them do. Worry is a form of fear that paralyzes people and their ability to take action. Worry expends energy, pollutes vision, and distracts people from their goals. Don't let others focus on worry or dwell on their past mistakes. Paint a vivid picture of the future. Give them hope, encouragement, and the tools to see themselves doing what they want or need to do. Help them get out of the past and into the future. Let them know that their past mistakes will not cloud their future potential.

Rate Your Vision
Add your score to page 182.

0	1	2	3	4	5	6	7	8	9	10
Poor		*Weak*			*Average*		*Strong*			*Perfect*

CHAPTER 29

EMPATHY:
COMPASSION CREATES FRIENDSHIP

If your emotional abilities aren't in hand, if you don't have
self-awareness, if you are not able to manage your distressing
emotions, if you can't have empathy and have effective
relationships, then no matter how smart you are, you are not
going to get very far.

— DANIEL GOLEMAN

The word *empathy* has both Latin and Greek roots. The two parts
of the word mean "to see through" and "the eye of the other." The
ability to see through the eye of another creates long-term charisma. When people know that you can see what they see, feel what
they feel, and hurt the way they hurt, then they will be willing to let
you influence them. Empathy is more than being aware of other
people's emotions and feelings. With it, you have the ability to ac-

knowledge and identify the inner state and well-being of other people. You can experience what they feel, know the emotions they are experiencing, and realize how those emotions would make you feel. This enables you to understand the attitudes, beliefs, and fears of others; you have entered their world as they know it. Empathy builds trust and respect, and long-term charisma is based on empathy. Charismatic people have the ability to pick up the subtle clues and the nonverbal signals indicating what is really happening inside another person.

Empathy is not sympathy, which is being able to relate to other people. Empathy is feeling for them and understanding them. Empathy is putting on their shoes and walking around in them. Learn how emotions work; practice reading people and using sincere empathy. Empathy is very difficult to learn from a book. We live in a self-absorbed world, and being empathetic is contrary to almost everything we've learned from society. Most people are not naturally empathetic; they have learned to be selfish and self-centered. Empathy is identifying with and understanding someone else's situation, feelings, and concerns in a realistic, sincere way. People will be surprised and drawn to you when you practice empathy.

When you accept the whole person unconditionally, you create empathy. You are able to accept the other person's strengths and triumphs, along with their weaknesses, failures, doubts, and fears. Developing empathy helps you feel better as a person and actually increases your happiness. We all have been told to put others first, but few people actually can do it. The people who can put others first become more charismatic. The people around them would do anything for them. Empathy will also increase your personal satisfaction and increase your productivity. Did you catch that? You are helping yourself while helping others and increasing your charisma.

BLIND SPOT

Empathy is a skill that we have never been taught. We have felt it and we have seen it in action, but most of us aren't sure how to implement it. We get so consumed with our world and our problems that we forget to learn how to care about other people. Yet those other people are the ones who are going to help us achieve our goals. One blind spot is failing to understand that pretending to care about other people is not showing empathy. Charismatic people have the ability to demonstrate sincere, genuine empathy. Another blind spot is thinking that sympathy is empathy. There is a difference.

APPLICATION

You can start implementing empathy in your daily contacts and conversations, but it takes some practice and evaluation. After every encounter, ask yourself what you did well and what you can do better next time. Try these steps to increase your empathy:

- Mentally prepare yourself to hear the other person's message.
- Listen with your ears, mind, and heart.
- Read their body language.
- Evaluate the true message being sent.
- Acknowledge the feelings and emotions being displayed.
- Practice taking on their perspective.
- Respond with empathy.

EXAMPLE

Nelson Mandela, the former president of South Africa, is a great example of empathy. He showed that he truly cared and always followed his values and principles. He knew the importance and power of empathy. He often said, "The best way to know a person is to walk a mile in their shoes." He spent 27 years in prison for his beliefs, and many people wanted him to take revenge on the powers that imprisoned him. He wanted to set things right, but he did not want to retaliate or to create more victims. He united a divided country using his example, his empathy, and his patience. He taught the people to seek understanding rather than revenge and to find points of agreement rather than points of contention and argument.

CHARISMA KEY

Although empathy takes some effort, perfecting this skill is worth every moment you spend. When you are truly empathetic, you will be more trustworthy and charismatic, and you will increase your productivity and inspire commitment in others. Our rushed modern life does not cultivate the mindset or skills of empathy. You need to look for opportunities to develop empathy. Just start off by asking yourself two questions during your conversations.

- ❧ "How would I feel if I were this person?"
- ❧ "Why is the person feeling that way?"

Practice this starting today. Find one person to whom you can demonstrate empathy, and show them you truly care.

Rate Your Empathy
Add your score to page 182.

0	1	2	3	4	5	6	7	8	9	10
Poor		*Weak*			*Average*		*Strong*			*Perfect*

CHAPTER 30

RESPECT:
GIVE IT TO GET IT

Respect a man, and he will do all the more.

— JOHN WOODEN

Long-term charisma is all about valuing people. It is about the respect you give to others, which breeds more charisma and influence. Respect is viral and highly contagious. Before you know it, respect has spread to everyone. When respect is high between two people or within a group, people have more trust, they are more open about feelings, and they are able to stay focused on the objective. Learn to build respect in others. The more respect you give, the more influential you become. Respect does not always come in an instant; sometimes it takes time to build. The point is that how people feel about you is in direct correlation to how you make them feel about themselves.

The key is to understand that, to radiate charisma, you have to be respected and give respect. It can be just that simple. You give it and you will get it. The respect you are earning is a combination of how you conduct yourself in all your affairs. When you show respect and character in all your dealings, people will see how you work with others and will talk about it. They also will be able to instantly sense the respect in you. Another word that applies is *honorable*. Be honorable and other people will trust, respect, and follow you.

If you are finding that people are not taking you, your message, or your company seriously, you could be looking at a red flag indicating a lack of respect. Because no respect means no influence, and definitely no charisma. The more respect you can earn, the more successful you will be in your communications.

A simple idea to implement is to be thankful for the things others do for you. People will always want to talk about two things: themselves or their problems. If you listen when people tell you their problems or issues, they will feel you are sympathetic, understanding, and respectful. This response helps you become a person who makes other people feel good about themselves, and it will go a long way toward increasing their respect for you and making them feel respected.

Respect can be as simple as the good old-fashioned manners your mother taught you. They are critical in all relationships, in the workplace, and in your ability to maintain charisma. Do you show appreciation? Do people feel good about themselves when they are around you? What do people really want in the workplace? It is a little respect. They want to feel empowered and to be rewarded for a job well done. They are tired of the lack of encouragement, favoritism, criticism, and never being asked for their opinion. Don't criticize anyone in front of others, demean the competition, or speak ill of your enemies. If you do, people will always wonder what you say about them when they aren't around.

BLIND SPOT

Showing a little common courtesy does not mean you are giving the person true respect. Not saying something mean or negative does not always show respect. That is the blind spot: You think you are showing admiration, respect, or concern, but the other person does not perceive you that way. A nice gesture is the right thing to do, but does it really convey true respect? Respect can be earned a little at a time, but lost in a moment. When showing true respect, you forget thinking about yourself. Make sure you are coming across as respectful to everyone you meet.

APPLICATION

Respect needs to be mutual. Once you show it, you can get it. And you can show it in many ways. Here are a few things you can start implementing when you are interacting with people:

- Always have integrity.
- Be dependable.
- Show long-term stability.
- Constantly practice your good manners.
- Be grateful to others.

EXAMPLE

One of the most respected leaders in business today is Michael Dell of Dell computers. While he was attending college, he started a computer hardware business in his room. It became so successful that he dropped out of college at 19 and started the company that eventually become Dell. He faced some setbacks and intense competition, but Dell computers has become one of the most profitable PC manufacturers in the world. Michael Dell continues to be very philanthropic. He radiates all the factors of respect. He has won countless awards. He has been voted both man of year and CEO of the year. When you are voted the best, it is because people respect you.

CHARISMA KEY

Today, practice treating everyone you meet with respect, and show them they are important to you whether they are the receptionist, the CEO, or the janitor. Everyone you meet can help you reach your goals and expand your influence. The best way to do this is to focus on asking people questions about themselves and answering their questions. Be sincere in your approach and show respect, and you will get respect back. Don't complain about anything, and don't criticize others for what they say or do. These simple things display your concern for another human being.

Rate Your Respect
Add your score to page 182.

0	1	2	3	4	5	6	7	8	9	10
Poor		*Weak*			*Average*		*Strong*			*Perfect*

EMPOWERING RESOURCES (LAWSOFCHARISMA.COM)

- Support articles
- Section support audio: "How to Motivate Yourself and Others Every Time"
- Section worksheet

SECTION FIVE

SUBCONSCIOUS TRIGGERS:
IT JUST FEELS RIGHT—OR WRONG

FABLE: THE FOX IN THE HOLE

A fox was running, jumping, and playing in a large field, enjoying one of the last days of autumn. As he sprang up and over a fence, he plunged headfirst into a hole that had been dug by a farmer who had been building a well. The farmer had found little water but left the large and gaping hole. In a panic the fox jumped and jumped, attempting to escape from his new prison, but always fell just short of the top. He was unable to spring himself free and was becoming incredibly fatigued and wet. Another fox walked by and stuck his face over the edge of the hole and asked the first fox what he was doing.

"Oh," said the fox in the hole, "haven't you heard? There's going to be a drought, and this will be the only water in all the land. I will let you join me and you'll be spared from the drought. Jump in now so you'll be saved too."

The second fox thought about this offer, and something just didn't feel right. A fellow fox was saying he wanted to help him and save his life, but every part of him was telling him to run.

"Come on," said the first fox, "jump in so you won't die." The fox in the hole was secretly planning to jump off the back of the second fox to his freedom and leave the other fox stuck in his place. The fox peering into the hole said, "I'll come back later to join you." Then he ran off, leaving the first fox stranded.

MEANING

People usually will follow their instinct when they are asked to do something. When things don't feel right, people often make up an excuse, lie, resist, or flee the situation. What types of feelings do you generate in others? Do they lie to you? Do they trust you? Do they like you? Do you repel them?

If you want to be ranked among charismatic people, you must know how to read people and how they read you. Most people are not educated in the art and science of human nature and social interaction. They just get a feeling when they're around you: Either it feels right or it feels wrong. When interacting with other people, you need to be able to manage not only your first impression, but every impression. They are judging you both consciously and subconsciously.

The final section of this book will teach you how to understand the subconscious triggers that determine how other people will respond to you. You will gain great confidence and charisma when you have the ability not only to read people, but to trigger the right feelings and moods during every encounter. Everything you do and say affects the emotions of others and how they feel about you.

Most people think if we give people all the logic, facts, and figures, things will work in our favor. *Wrong!* We do have a logical side, but studies show that we are extremely emotional. Our subconscious mind and emotions are huge factors in our decisions and in how we feel and treat other people. Did you know that up to 95 percent of all influence depends on a subconscious trigger?[1] This means that inclinations—"It just seems right," "It feels good to me," "I don't trust that guy"—are based on subconscious, emotional reactions. This 95 percent of subconscious thought and emotional feeling occurs in the unconscious mind without our awareness. In other words, our conscious awareness of reality is the result of subconscious triggers.

A subconscious trigger is a feeling that says "I like/don't like this person." Everything you do or say can trigger a response (good or bad) in others. It could be your word choice, your tone of voice, your gestures, or your appearance; it could also be the atmosphere, the effect of music, or the mood of the audience. When you become charismatic, you will be able to read people, find patterns in their behavior, and know which emotions you are creating. Human behavior is usually predictable; we all have certain triggers or knee-jerk reactions. Long-term charisma depends on knowing these triggers and how they work.

Do you see the power of understanding why people do what they do and getting inside their minds? How do others really feel and think about you? What if you knew the questions and objections brewing in their minds? What if you knew their main motivators or their feelings? What if you could identify whether they are telling the truth or lying to you? As we get into subconscious triggers, understand that, as humans, we spend little or no time processing the constant bombardment of information around us. We don't have time to process everything, so we develop these mental shortcuts. We tend to follow our feelings, even if we don't admit doing so. We always respond more to gut instincts, intuition, and other emotionally based triggers than we do to logic and reasoning. We just want to feel right about things. We are emotional, subconscious decision makers with a touch of logic.

As you develop charisma, you are going to realize that most of your influence will operate at a level below conscious thought. When you ask others why they thought a certain person was charismatic, you will get many standard responses, but the reality is that

---

1. Joseph Sugarman, Ron Hugher, and Dick Hafer, *Triggers: 30 Sales Tools You Can Use to Control the Mind of Your Prospect to Motivate, Influence and Persuade* (Delstar Pub, 1999), p. 9.

they just felt the charisma. This knowledge will empower you to influence others and get them in the right state of mind. You will have better relationships, become more charismatic, master the ability to influence people, and improve your income.

We will be discussing these five categories of subconscious triggers:

- *Verbal:* Words, rate, and inflection
- *Nonverbal:* Gestures, space, and movement
- *State*: Emotion, mood, and feelings
- *Appearance:* Dress, accessories, and attraction
- *Triggers That Repel:* What causes resistance

CHAPTER 31

VERBAL PRESENTATION:
IT IS *HOW YOU SAY IT*

We judge others by their voice. If you sound either uncertain and timid or arrogant and demanding, your ability to gain charisma will falter. Your voice is your calling card: It must exude confidence, courage, and conviction. Charismatic voices have a soothing volume, varied emphases, good articulation, and a pleasing pitch. Your voice will either connect you with your audience or disconnect with them on a subconscious level.

What does your voice trigger in people? Do you use repelling words? How you package your words and how you say them can create energy and excitement. The right words will captivate your audience, and the wrong ones will drive them away. The right words in the right tone can help you create a strong connection, and you will become more influential. Your voice must be interesting and easy to listen to if you are going to help, rather than hinder, your ability to gain charisma and influence others.

The more you learn about your verbal presentation, the more you will be able to maintain charisma and influence. The words you use do affect attitudes, beliefs, and emotions. Charismatic people understand the importance of using language in ways that evoke vivid thoughts, feelings, and actions in their audiences. I assume that you know the basics of the English language, but you should strive to learn how to use it to your advantage. You will become more adaptable, able to customize your influence, and easier to understand.

To create an effective verbal presentation, you need to understand the following critical aspects of verbal packaging:

1. *Word Choice:* Each word you use has an impact on your charisma. Words help people form thoughts, feelings, and attitudes toward a person or subject. When you master the use of words, you will become more credible and convincing. If you don't, you will repel people and come across as weak and ineffective. Proper words and language will vary from setting to setting, from person to person, and from event to event. One size does not fit all. Word choice can also be essential to defuse emotional situations and get people to accept your point of view and enhance your charisma.

2. *Rate of Speech:* The rate of speech is how fast you speak. Speeches delivered at a fast rate are rated more influential and charismatic than those presented at slow or even moderate speeds, because people who speak faster appear more competent and knowledgeable. When your overall rate is fast, people pay more attention and have less time to think of other things. Obviously, you need to vary your rate of speech, or people will become tense and tune out. Be careful if your rate is always fast with no variation; you will be judged as less sincere and more self-centered. Slow your rate down when you have something important or serious to say or want to appear thoughtful. Increase your rate when you want to create excitement and energy. During a one-on-one encounter, match the other person's rate initially and slowly increase your rate during the presentation.

3. *Vocal Fillers:* You are probably using these and don't know it. Most of us feel we don't have a problem with vocal fillers,

and most of us are wrong. You know what I am talking about: "um," "er," "uh," or even "ya know." These types of fillers can destroy your presentation, annoy people, hurt your credibility, and make listeners tense. A few fillers here and there are not that big a deal, but most people tend to violate this rule excessively. You probably have heard people with their own distinctive way of filling the silence between thoughts. Sometimes you will hear them repeat the first two or three words of a sentence until their brain catches up. Others might say "okay" or "dude" at the end of every sentence, as if they're checking to see whether you're still listening. Work to eliminate all vocal fillers from your verbal presentations.

4. *Pitch and Inflection: Pitch* is the level of your voice frequency. When you have a high pitch, you are judged as nervous, excited, or vulnerable. A low pitch tends to show more strength, confidence, and assurance. A lower voice is usually considered to be more believable, sincere, and trustworthy. Pitch is the first thing we judge when we decide whether someone's voice is pleasant or irritating. Varying your pitch will also help listeners stay more alert and attentive, and you won't sound monotonous. *Inflection* is when you alter the pitch or tone of your voice. You will notice that influential people use inflection in their voices to show confidence and authority. At the end of their sentences, they will usually inflect downward. Listen to your own inflection. Most people who aren't confident or show doubt tend to inflect upward at the end of their sentences.

5. *Volume:* This aspect of speaking is easy to understand, but often abused. You only have three options: too soft, too loud, or just right. If your audience can't hear you, then maintaining charisma or being influential is very difficult. When the audience has to strain to hear you, they often will give up trying to listen. On the other hand, some people tend to yell or speak in a very high volume, causing tension and aggravation. Plant someone in the back of the room to rate your volume, or ask a friend on the phone whether your volume sounds good. Raising your volume for impact is not as effec-

tive as lowering your voice. When you want the audience to really lean forward and listen, try speaking a bit lower.

6. *Articulation:* When you are talking to someone or delivering a speech, clearly articulate every phrase and word. A clear and coherent presentation radiates congruence. Good articulation conveys competence and credibility. Even a little sloppy articulation suggests a lack of education or laziness. Another practical reason to have good pronunciation is simply to make it easy for the audience to follow you, pay attention to your message, and understand it. People are more likely to be won over by your message and feel your charisma when you are easy to understand.

7. *Silence:* Is silence really part of your verbal presentation? Yes, it is. A well-placed pause can grab attention at any time and with any audience. They can sense something important is about to happen. Pauses let the audience mentally prepare for what you are about to say and allow you to emphasize your point. Use intentional pauses for the topics you consider the most important. Not only does a pause increase comprehension, but it also helps you gather your thoughts. Use pauses to create attention, emphasis, and mood. As you come to the pause, be sure to keep your pitch a little high; this builds suspense and gives momentum to the pause. Inflecting your pitch downward will defeat the purpose of the pause and create a feeling of resolution instead of suspense.

TAKEAWAY

Does your voice work for you or against you? Because of the many nuances, feelings, and moods you can convey with your voice, record your voice and listen to it. I know that can be a little painful, but the exercise is worth it. What does your voice project? Do you sound compelling and convincing? Besides the message, listen to your pitch, your pace, your volume, your tone, and your articulation. Effective use of this vocal variety catches and holds other people's attention. If you don't like how you sound, take a deep breath and find a solution. Many people do not like their own voices. Make sure that you listen for specific aspects that you don't like, instead of the blanket reaction of not liking anything about your voice. Focus on the exact aspects of your voice that you'd like to change, then make one improvement at a time. A handy digital recorder may prove to be your best coach.

CHAPTER 32

NONVERBAL COMMUNICATION:
GESTURES TRUMP WORDS

To captivate and mesmerize their audiences, charismatic people express themselves in positive nonverbal ways. During each encounter, charismatic people are careful what gestures they use and don't use. Their gestures look spontaneous, but they are well planned and practiced. Think of your body as a prop. You are telling a story and keeping the attention of your audience. Make sure your gestures are positive and come across as natural and purposeful.

Not only do charismatic people use nonverbal gestures in the right way, they also have the ability to read and interpret the nonverbal gestures of others. When you are able to read people in this way, you can obtain the knowledge you need to adjust yourself and your presentation based on what you are reading. When you are aware of your own body language, you can synchronize your nonverbals to create instant likeability and rapport. You can create positive subconscious triggers. If you don't have control of your nonverbals, you could come across as flustered, nervous, or out of control.

Let's look at the different parts of the body and how different gestures can be perceived as either positive, negative, or deceptive. Remember you are looking for clusters, that is, two or three of these nonverbals going on at the same time. A single nonverbal sign does not exactly define what is going on.

EYES

Make sure there is plenty of light for your audience to see your eyes. Never wear sunglasses when you are attempting to gain charisma or influence. As for reading your audience, eyes can give you mountains of information. When you learn to read eyes, you can detect deception and determine what someone is feeling. When someone is attempting deception, look for the following:

- Decreased or forced eye contact
- Increased blinking
- Pupils dilating

HANDS

The hands are a great indicator of what others are thinking and feeling and how you're being perceived. Clenching your hands in a fist detracts from you presence and your message and indicates anger, aggression, or tension. If you are standing with your hands close to or across your body, this is a closed posture and does not open people up. If you place your hands flat on the table in front of you, you may be sending a signal that you agree. On the other hand, placing your hands on your hips may express defiance or dominance. When someone is attempting deception, look for the following with respect to the hands:

- Decreased hand movements
- Hiding parts of the face with the hands
- Palms becoming sweaty

LEGS

A person's legs pointing in your direction often indicates interest. On the flip side, if the feet are pointed away, you have lost the listener. Crossed legs while someone is standing could mean the person is feeling awkward or uneasy. Tapping a foot means the person is either wishing you would shut up or a sign of boredom. When legs are tucked up under someone's rear end it could indicate that the person is feeling comfortable in your presence and enjoying the visit. When someone is attempting deception, look for the following with their legs:

- Crossing and uncrossing
- Wiggling or tapping
- Feet underneath the chair

SHOULDERS AND ARMS

Just like the feet, if the other person's shoulders are aligned with your shoulders, you have made a connection. When a group of people are standing together, their shoulder alignment will tend to look more like a circle when there is a connection. Crossing their arms could be a sign of rejection. We know that, if they start picking or pulling at their arm (or hands), they are starting to become nervous. If you see a shoulder shrug, that is also a disconnect. When someone is attempting deception, look for the following with their arms or shoulders:

- Crossing arms
- Shoulders turned away
- Shoulder shrug

HEAD

The head is also a great indicator of what is going on inside a person. This is the one body part that most people attempt to control during a conversation because they are the most aware of it. When the head starts to tilt a little, you are starting to grab the person's attention. (Animals do this when they are trying to gather more information.) Supporting the head with the hands means you have lost the connection and could be a sign of lack of interest. When people get nervous, more blood flows to the head, and you will see increased touching to any part of the head, changes in the color of the skin, and/or an increase/decrease in movement. When someone is attempting deception, look for the following with their head:

- Biting lip
- Dry mouth
- Ears or nose turns red

BODY

The amount of movement is a big indicator. When two people are connected, the movement increases; when there is a disconnect, physical movement will be minimal. Overall gestures and body movement will decrease when you have lost your connection with the person. When you are making someone nervous, you will see a change in posture. Just watch the spine. Either leaning away or sitting a little too erect would be a disconnect. If the spine or even their hips are pointed toward you, you are starting to make the connection. When someone is attempting deception, look for the following with their body:

- Increase in perspiration
- More mechanical movements
- Physically moving back

TOUCH

Touch is a powerful nonverbal trigger that can help or hurt your ability to connect because most people like to be touched. You need to be aware and careful of a small percentage of the population who dislikes being touched in any way. In most instances, however, touch can help put people at ease and make them more receptive to you and your ideas.

Touching is not grabbing people; I am talking about a non-threatening touch to a person's arm, shoulder, back, or hand. Touch makes us feel appreciated and liked.

In one instance of touching, however, most people can make or break the connection: the handshake. How you shake hands will trigger how people remember you. Your handshake tells a story about you; it dictates a first impression that could last forever. A good handshake will make someone feel appreciated and connected to you. Yet some people refuse to shake hands. Even a slight reluctance to shake hands can put a damper on your ability to win friends. A bad handshake can set you back an hour in rapport building. Make sure you shake the correct way. Every handshake you give should be a little different. Learn to mirror the other person's handshake and customize it to the person, culture, and situation.

What are the big complaints about handshakes?

- Crushing
- Wimpy
- Excessive pumps
- Sweaty
- Finger squeeze
- Cold hand

What makes a great handshake?

- Shoulders aligned
- Mirroring their strength
- Rise if seated
- A sincere smile and eye contact
- Three or four pumps
- Arm completely extended

TAKEAWAY

Practice learning to read people in every situation throughout the day. Turn the audio off on a movie or sitcom to get a better read on how to interpret body language. Be more aware of your own body movements and nonverbal behavior. Learning body language takes some effort, but the rewards will last a lifetime. Take note of the following gestures. Then implement the connectors and decrease your use of the disconnectors.

Nonverbals that show you are connecting:

- Slightly tilted head
- Head starting to nod
- Posture relaxed
- Leaning forward
- Starting to smile
- Increase in eye contact
- Mirroring your movements
- The other person touches you
- Open palms
- Legs uncrossed

Nonverbals that show you are starting to disconnect:

- Head on hands
- Sweating
- Shoulders turned away
- Rigid posture
- Movement becoming more mechanical
- Crossing arms
- Crossing legs
- Biting lip
- Ears turning red
- Rubbing nose

CHAPTER 33

EMOTIONAL STATES:
UNDERSTANDING FEELINGS AND MOODS

Charismatic people know there is a fine line between logic and
emotion. To influence someone, you have to have both, but be
aware that people's emotions will override their logic every time.
You may be able to form a logical argument, but you must understand emotions if you want to become more charismatic. Very few
really understand how emotional states, feelings, subconscious
triggers, and moods affect other people and your ability to maintain charisma and influence.

   Logic tends to be temporary, whereas emotion will carry your
message into the future. Emotion inspires us to take action,
whereas logic justifies those actions. Most people can't really distinguish between logic and emotion. Even identifying the many emotions you feel throughout a day is difficult. People can't predict
what emotions they will feel, how long they will feel them, and how
strong the emotions will be. They just sense whether you and/or

your message makes them feel good or bad. Your goal is either to change the emotional state of others if it's running against you or to maintain it if it is working for you.

Moods affect every aspect of our being. We are not even aware most of the time that our moods affect our thinking, our judgment, and our willingness to be influenced. Think about it: Sometimes you are very willing to be influenced, and at other times you will resist no matter what. When the people you are trying to influence are in a good mood, they are easier to influence. The opposite is also true. If they are in a bad mood, they tend to increase their resistance, making them harder to influence. Charismatic people can create the right mood at the right time. They can put people in a happy state. When people are feeling happy, they tend to think more positive thoughts and to retrieve good experiences from memory. When they are in a negative or foul mood, they tend to think unhappy thoughts and to retrieve negative information from memory.

Your ability to change people's moods and handle emotions is a critical factor in your ability to maintain charisma. Do the emotions they are feeling fit your message? Are their emotions helping or hurting your ability to influence? Is their mood detracting from your charisma? Are you dealing with someone who can switch emotions suddenly and knock you off guard? Let's look at some common emotions and what they mean to you when you try to influence others.

EMOTIONS THAT DETRACT FROM YOUR CHARISMA AND DECREASE YOUR ABILITY TO INFLUENCE

Anger

Anger is a sign that something is out of line. Anger is also known as a secondary emotion. In other words, what people say they are angry about and what they are really upset about are usually two different things. You can help decrease a person's anger by finding out the real reason for the anger. Ask for the person's help, opinions, or advice. This request will usually diffuse their anger or even help change their demeanor. Don't try to use anger to make a point or evoke a reaction. The attempt will usually backfire on you.

Worry

When someone is worried or preoccupied with something occurring now or that could happen in the future, your ability to change their mood or influence them decreases. Worry causes people to feel nervous, uneasy, or anxious. Worry can be referred to as a negative vision of the future. You can therefore help your audience by bringing them back to reality, back to the now. Worry will subside when you can substitute positive images for their negative ones. Another way to decrease worry is by helping them make a decision. Worry decreases when decisions are made.

Fear

Fear is anxiety or tension caused by a sense of danger or apprehension. The possibility of harm can be real, but the feeling is usually the result of an overactive imagination. Fear motivates us and moves us away from perceived unpleasant circumstances or certain danger. Logic rarely helps in reducing fear. The key to understanding fear is to realize that it has been learned from a past experience. Remember that fear is very real to people. Make sure when they are afraid that you can provide a solution. Then your job as a great influencer is to help them feel capable of overcoming their fear.

EXTERNAL FACTORS THAT AFFECT EMOTIONS

Now that you understand a few critical emotions, we need to talk about the external factors that can change other people's perception about you or their surroundings. External factors can change perceptions, moods, and emotions. This phenomenon is not something your audience can quantify. Let's learn how we can change other people's state of mind and how they are feeling.

Music

Music is closely tied to our emotions, moods, and feelings. You probably still remember that favorite song played during the dance with your high school sweetheart. Instantaneously, you are transported back and can feel some of the same emotions. Music has a powerful pull on us and triggers instant moods and memories. Understand that music can trigger good or bad feelings and good or bad memories. We know music can lull you to sleep, give you more energy, make you feel more romantic, or even make you want to smack the person next to you.

Smell

Our sense of smell can evoke memories and moods more quickly than music. The right smell can make you feel comfortable or like you have been friends with someone forever. The wrong smell will do the opposite. It will repel others, make them feel uncomfortable, and cause them not to like you or even want to be around you. One of the big complaints regarding smell is excessive perfume or cologne. Do you really think you need that much? You want to smell clean, but you don't need to use all the smelly stuff (at least in the business world). A strange smell can put someone in the wrong state of mind for you to be able to influence them.

Colors

Colors matter more than you imagine. Colors can trigger a mood, a feeling, or an attitude. They do so at a subconscious level; we don't even realize it is happening. The response to certain colors can differ from culture to culture, but colors are powerful. Companies spend millions of dollars every year just to decide on the colors to use on new product packaging. We all have automatic color triggers, as well as hidden associations and feelings about various colors. Color impacts our thinking and our reactions. Learn to choose the right colors for the right experience and the right state of mind.

TAKEAWAY

Get a better feel about how your surroundings and external stimuli help or hurt your ability to maintain charisma or become more influential. When you can master these skills, you will be able to produce the desired feelings, emotions, and responses in your audience. You can learn to create the experience you want to generate and help them feel more open, more comfortable, and more willing to be influenced

CHAPTER 34

PHYSICAL APPEARANCE:
JUDGE NOT (YEAH, RIGHT!)

Does appearance matter? We are all taught *not* to judge one other by appearance, but we all do. The right judgment about you will increase your charisma and influence, and the wrong judgment means your ability to influence and your charisma just took a nosedive. Do you look athletic, tall, fat, or fit? Physique has always been associated with charisma. The shape and look of your face and body will also affect judgments. Every aspect of your appearance changes how you are judged. I know this fact is not fair, but it is time to deal with reality.

Here are some things we know about physical appearance:

- Adult faces with baby-type characteristics are judged as honest.
- Excess weight decreases credibility.

- High foreheads increase the perception of intelligence.
- Old hairstyles decrease your rapport.
- Taller people are more credible and have increased power.
- Facial hair decreases trust.
- Slouching posture disconnects people from you.
- Larger than normal ears decreases perception of intelligence.
- White teeth are rated as more attractive.

Your appearance is judged by both positive and negative characteristics. Your positive traits cause people to upgrade their overall perception of you. When you have a pleasing appearance, people automatically associate you with traits like trust and intelligence. Interestingly, you don't want to look too perfect or too handsome or beautiful. If you are drop-dead gorgeous or handsome, connecting with people can be hard because they might feel you are way out of their league. Slight physical flaws relax our defenses and we feel more connected to someone. I am not talking about glaring irregularities, but about minor things like slight balding, a small scar, or even an oddly shaped nose,

What is being judged?

- Overall appearance
- Weight
- Grooming
- Hair
- Accessories
- Clothing

You can increase your charisma with physical appearance in many different ways. (Even your personality can be either attractive or ugly.) Attractiveness lies in the simple things that many people don't even consider, like being in shape and watching your weight, picking the right clothes to wear, paying attention to your accessories, and having a good-looking hairstyle. Keep track of the style. Styles can change fast, and, if we ignore the fashion of the day, our charismatic ability may decrease.

CLOTHES

What are you telling people by the way you dress? Many people don't care how they dress or look, and their disregard shows; many care too much and that overconcern also shows. Clothing will either increase or decrease your credibility and ability to influence. Do you need a tailor? Do you need a consultant? Are you holding onto a style that no longer exists? The wrong clothing will rob you of potential charisma. If you are out of touch, why would someone listen to you? You don't have to be cutting-edge in your style, but your clothes should never detract from your appearance. Pay attention to trends and to the expectations of your audience. Make sure your clothes are comfortable and make you feel good (mentally and physically). When you look good, you feel good.

BEYOND APPEARANCE

Maybe you can't change much about your looks, but you can pay close attention to your immediate surroundings, such as your office, accessories, and external symbols. External objects and accessories also affect people's perceptions of your authority and charisma. Make sure you check your surroundings to see whether you are sending the right message: the type of watch you wear, the briefcase or purse you carry, objects on your desk, or even the type of glasses you wear. Are your shoes shined or scuffed, in style or out of style? How professional is your Web site, your business cards, your letterhead, and your office décor? What do people see when they come into your office? Is it clean and organized? Does it feel professional?

TAKEAWAY

You may think that people are not acting fairly when they judge you on so many factors beyond your character, your competence, and your message. You cannot change or control many of these things, but look to the future and fix the things you can fix. Realize that no one will be able to change 100 percent of the things discussed in this chapter. The more you can master or fix, however, the easier it will be for you to develop charisma. Pick one thing you can change or adjust today. Changing even one thing will enhance your image and appearance and increase your ability to influence.

CHAPTER 35

HOW YOU REPEL PEOPLE:
DON'T DRIVE THEM AWAY

Do you repel people? Most people would say no, although most of us do things that drive people away. No doubt you have met people who just rubbed you the wrong way. They repelled you, you did not like them, and you didn't want to be around them. You probably never told them what they did wrong or how they made you feel; you just left and hoped you would never see them again. When people are repelled by you, you can't have much influence over them, and they are not likely to view you as charismatic. What mannerism or things are you doing that turn people off, cause them to run away, and drive down your charisma IQ? For example, do you appear nervous, upset, or tense? Charismatic people help other people relax and put them at ease.

You can be offending and upsetting people and not even know you're doing it. You may think you're just being friendly or even concerned, but you are doing things that will attract or repel others.

I am not here to sugarcoat the point: In my studies, I often get to talk to people after you have (or someone else has) tried to connect with them or tried to influence them. They don't complain to you, but they complain to me about the things you are doing and don't even know you are doing. Others will be nice by not telling you, but not knowing what you are doing to repel others will cost you money and charisma.

Here are some of the complaints and things you could be doing that repel others:

- *Talking Too Much:* Having the gift of gab, or being able to make small talk with anyone you meet, can definitely be used to your advantage, but watch yourself. How can you influence others if you are always talking? It will be very annoying to your audience if they sense that you like hearing yourself talk more than listening to their wants, needs, or concerns.

- *Showing How Much You Know:* Many times, in our impatience to impress our audience with our knowledge and wisdom, we simply list the countless reasons why they should do what you want them to do. When you simply spit out all the features or overpersuade, you give your audience no room to ask questions or to make a decision. You come across as forceful, aggressive, and obnoxious.

- *Getting Too Friendly Too Fast:* Gone are the days of picking out something in a person's office and talking about it to be friendly. People see right through your attempts to befriend them, and the attempt usually will backfire on you. Research tells us that the majority of people do not appreciate unsolicited small talk, and many find it offensive. People buy from those who understand their wants and needs.

- *Getting Too Comfortable Too Fast:* You want to feel at ease so that you can put the other person at ease. Perhaps you just may want to get to know the person, but what you are doing is repelling. When you touch things on the desk, move something special to a different spot, or even sit down in their own personal chair, you can create resentment. Respect their things and they will respect you.

❧ *Too Old-School:* Are you coming across as an old-school persuader who is using techniques that are so lame, so offensive, and so outdated that they repel the other person? Are you stuck on using some of those closing skills that should have been banned years ago for cheesiness? Another way to disconnect relates to how you handle their objections, brushing them aside with well-worn phrases and tactics. You have heard the objection before, but how you handle it causes you to be judged as arrogant and condescending.

❧ *Proxemics:* Proxemics is the study of spatial separation. On a practical basis, how close can you get to someone before the person becomes tense and uneasy? The distance you keep or don't keep when influencing someone communicates a message. You must respect personal space, or you will make others feel uncomfortable. When we sit at a table or across from a desk, we each draw invisible lines of our perceived personal space. When you violate these invisible territorial lines, you create tension. We all have regions or areas where we permit others to enter or prevent them from entering.

TAKEAWAY

These mistakes are silent charisma killers. Most people will never say anything to you that will alert you to the fact they are being repelled. They are more comfortable lying to you so that they don't hurt your feelings. They walk away and simply never deal with you again. This obstacle is such a killer because we don't even realize we're doing it. Here are other things you could be doing that repel people:

❧ Exaggerating the details or features

❧ Asking unnecessary questions

❧ Coming across as too smooth

- Arguing or trying to prove you are right
- Annoying persistence
- Lack of enthusiasm
- Poor follow-through
- Negative attitude
- Being one-sided with your facts
- Exerting high-pressure tactics
- Exaggeration or hype
- Insincerity with your connectivity
- Showing any sign of deception
- Sense your fear of rejection
- Making lame excuses

SUBCONSCIOUS RESOURCES (LAWSOFCHARISMA.COM)

- Support articles
- Section support audio: "Mood Matters: Emotions That Hinder Persuasion"
- Section worksheet

CONCLUSION

FABLE: THE FIGHTING BROTHERS

There was a family that consisted of all sons, who spent most of the day fighting and quarreling with one another. They were always competing with each other, and each always felt that he had to win the contest. The mother and father tried to get their sons to be at peace with one another and quit their fighting because it was taking its toll on everyone, especially the parents. The father wanted to find a way to get his sons to be on the same team.

One day the fighting and quarreling were much more violent and disturbing than ever. It was going on all day, and by the evening the father was at his wit's end. He knew that he had to take action. He lined all the sons up on the back porch and demanded that they go out into the woods. He told them to gather as many sticks as they could carry. They all thought it was a contest and raced into the woods to gather as many sticks as possible and bring them back to their father.

When they arrived on the back porch, they all wanted to see who had won the contest. They were surprised when their father asked them to hold out their bundle of sticks. Whoever could break the whole bundle would be the winner, he told them. With all their might, they grunted, groaned, and tried to break the bundles, but, of course, no one was able to do so. Then the father grabbed the smallest bundle and gave each son a single stick.

The father asked the sons whether they could each break an

individual branch. They all were able to break the single stick with ease.

"My sons," he declared, "you have learned two valuable lessons today. First, if you stick together as brothers, you will accomplish more as a team than as individuals. Second, any task that is too big for any one of you can be broken down into smaller pieces. Then you can all accomplish it together."

MEANING

- When you tap into your charisma, you will attract many people to you. As you gather people and build teams and create synergy, you will become unbreakable, have unlimited power, and then have the resources to achieve your goals and make the world a better place. The bottom line is simple: We know that when we work together, we can accomplish more.

- As a whole, everything you have learned in this book could be overwhelming if you attempt to do all of it at once. Break the content down into individual skills, and master one skill a day or even one skill a week. Then by the end of the month or year, you will have broken down the large goal (the bundle of sticks) and you'll have a much firmer grasp of the tools of charisma.

WHAT'S NEXT?

What we learn to do, we learn by doing.

— Aristotle

It's not what you are going to do, but it's what you are doing

now that counts.

— Napoleon Hill

Charisma is a lifetime pursuit. Be careful you don't confuse popularity or the number of friends you have with charisma. Even if you can influence people to do things, you do not necessarily have long-term influence over them. You will never arrive at truly mastering this critical life skill—it is a lifetime pursuit. So keep working on your charisma. The more tools you learn, the more successful you are going to be.

Some of the skills we talked about may come naturally to you. Some will need a little practice. Others will be completely foreign to you and require your concentrated effort.

To win the race (to achieve your goals), you must start running. I was once getting ready to run in a half-marathon, not something you would take lightly. I was doing my preliminary stretching when I saw a T-shirt that revealed a great truth: "The challenge is not finishing; the challenge is starting." Make up your mind to start the race, and then you will know that you are moving toward your goal of finishing. You can come up with all the excuses you want, but none of them will bring you success or happiness. Practice these techniques everyday. The first time you try anything, it might feel a little awkward or might not even work. Stick to the plan, stick to the race, and you will see success.

FINAL RESOURCES (LAWSOFCHARISMA.COM)

- Additional articles
- Support audio: "The Brickwall of Resistance"
- Section worksheet

Rate Your Charisma Skills/Traits

___ Confidence	___ People skills
___ Congruence	___ Influence
___ Optimism	___ Story mastery
___ Positive power	___ Eye contact
___ Energy and balance	___ Listening
___ Humor/happiness	___ Rapport
___ Self-discipline	___ Inspire
___ Competence	___ Esteem
___ Intuition	___ Credibility
___ Purpose	___ Motivate
___ Integrity	___ Goodwill
___ Courage	___ Vision
___ Creativity	___ Empathy
___ Focus	___ Respect
___ Presentation skills	

RESEARCH

Chapter 1: Passion: The Transfer of Pure Energy

When two persuaders (with very different incomes) are compared with similar intelligence, similar core competence, and the same persuasion skills, the difference between the high and low income is usually passion. [Kurt W. Mortensen, *Persuasion IQ: The 10 Skills You Need to Get Exactly What You Want* (New York: AMACOM, 2008).]

How are charismatic people described by their followers? In terms of awe, inspiration, and empowerment. [O. Behling and J. M. McFillen, "A Syncretical Model of Charismatic/Transformational Leadership," *Group & Organization Management* (June 1996): 21.]

Enthusiasm and emotions are catching. [James M. Kouzes and Barry Z. Posner, *The Leadership Challenge*, 4th ed. (San Francisco: Jossey-Bass, 2008), p. 144.]

When you have passion, you have a sense of mission that drives you, stimulates your imagination, and motivates you to higher levels of achievement. [Kurt W. Mortensen, *Persuasion IQ: The 10 Skills You Need to Get Exactly What You Want* (New York: AMACOM, 2008).]

Chapter 2: Confidence: Conviction Is Contagious

Charismatic people project a powerful, confident, dynamic presence. [Bernard M. Bass, *Bass & Stogdill's Handbook of Leadership*, 3rd ed. (New York: Free Press, 1990), p. 190.]

Confidence is at a 10-year low. [Global Leadership Forecast, a biannual study conducted by Development Dimensions International (DDI) (http://www.ddiworld.com/about/pr_releases_ch.asp? id = 181).]

Charismatic people display complete confidence in the correctness of their positions and in their capabilities. [Bernard M. Bass, *Bass & Stogdill's Handbook of Leadership*, 3rd ed. (New York: Free Press, 1990), p. 190.]

When charismatic leaders feel discouraged or face imminent failure they don't make those feelings public. [Bernard M. Bass, *Bass & Stogdill's Handbook of Leadership*, 3rd ed. (New York: Free Press, 1990), p. 190.]

Arrogance is the number one complaint against managers. [Heather Johnson, "Overbearing Arrogance. (ThermoStat)," *Training*, 39, 12 (December 2002): 18(1). (Senior management posts, interviewing techniques, brief article.)]

Chapter 3: Congruence: Actions Versus Intention

The wrong cues or gestures can lead to impressions that the speaker is not so competent. [P. D. Blanck and R. Rosenthal, "Nonverbal Behavior in the Courtroom. In R. S. Feldman (Ed.), *Applications of Nonverbal Behavioral Theories and Research* (New York: Lawrence Erlbaum, 1992), pp. 89–118).]

Your gestures can lead to judgments that you lack confidence and credibility. [P. D. Blanck and R. Rosenthal, "Nonverbal Behavior in the Courtroom. In R. S. Feldman (Ed.), *Applications of Nonverbal Behavioral Theories and Research* (Hillsdale, N.J.: Lawrence Erlbaum, 1992), pp. 89–118).]

Nonverbal behaviors affect impressions of the sociability and attractiveness of a speaker. [J. K. Burgoon, T. Birk, and M. Pfau, "Nonverbal Behaviors, Persuasion, and Credibility," *Human Communication Research*, 17 (1990): 140–169.]

Gestures that convey less immediacy (lack of eye contact, leaning back, reduced proximity) communicate that you don't like others. [J. K. Burgoon, T. Birk, and M. Pfau, "Nonverbal Behaviors, Persuasion, and Credibility," *Human Communication Research*, 17 (1900): 140–169.]

Chapter 4: Optimism: Adjust Attitudes

Adopting an optimistic outlook early in life will add years to your life. [David Snowdon, *Aging with Grace: What the Nun Study Teaches Us About Leading Longer, Healthier, and More Meaningful Lives* (New York: Bantam, 2002).]

Optimism leads to the development and maintenance of better and stronger social networks and social support. [Copyright 2003 W. H. White Publications, Inc. "Be Optimistic; Improve Your Health," "Positive Thinking, Faster Recovery," "Power of Positive Thinking Extends . . . to Aging."]

People that have an optimistic outlook on life have demonstrated higher levels of motivation, persistence, and performance. [S. E. Taylor and J. D. Brown, "Illusion and Well-being: A Social Psychological Perspective on Mental Health," *Psychological Bulletin*, 103 (1988): 193–210.]

Belief in good luck produces a positive impression that causes feelings of optimism and confidence. [M. E. P. Seligman and P. Schulman, "Explanatory Style as a Predictor of Productivity and Quitting Among Life Insurance Sales Agents," *Journal of Personality and Social Psychology*, 50 (1986): 832–838.]

Pessimistic people give up twice as fast as optimistic people. [Ibid.]

Chapter 5: Positive Power: Force Is *Not* Charisma

Expert power is manifest in information, knowledge, and wisdom. [Bernard M. Bass, *Bass & Stogdill's Handbook of Leadership*, 3rd ed. (New York: Free Press, 1990), p. 233.]

Deep inside each person is a desire to have power and incite reactions in others. [Floyd Allport, *Social Psychology* (New York: Houghton-Mifflin, 1999).]

Charisma, like leadership, is a function of one's position. [Bernard M. Bass, *Bass & Stogdill's Handbook of Leadership*, 3rd ed. (Free Press, 1990), p. 185.]

Individuals asking for contributions for law enforcement and health-care campaigns gathered more donations when wearing sheriffs' and nurses' uniforms than when they just dressed normally. [L. Bickman, "The Social Power of a Uniform," *Journal of Applied Social Psychology*, (1974): 47–61.]

Pedestrians at a traffic signal committed more violations when they witnessed an experimenter who was dressed to represent a person of high social status commit a violation. [Bernard M. Bass, *Bass & Stogdill's Handbook of Leadership*, 3rd ed. (New York: Free Press, 1990), p. 171.]

Chapter 6: Energy and Balance: Vibrant Well-Being

Those who are charismatic have high levels of energy and are actively involved. [Bernard M. Bass, *Bass & Stogdill's Handbook of Leadership*, 3rd ed. (New York: Free Press, 1990), p. 207.]

Having friends and good relationships makes you healthier. [Dorothy Foltz-Gray, "The Laughing Cure: Why This Couple Will Never Get Sick. (Good Health From Laughter and Enjoyment)," *Prevention*, 50, 10 (October 1998): 92(9).]

Positive social ties increase our ability to fight disease. [E. Bachen, S. Manuck, M. Muldoon, S. Cohen, and B. Rabin, "Effects of Dispositional Optimism on Immunologic Responses to Laboratory Stress," 1991, unpublished data.]

Religion and prayer decrease your chances of getting cancer and heart disease. [*International Journal of Psychiatry in Medicine*, October 1997.]

Chapter 7: Humor and Happiness: It Comes from Within

Being cheerful and having a happy disposition is always associated with charisma.

[Bernard M. Bass, *Bass & Stogdill's Handbook of Leadership*, 3rd ed. (New York: Free Press, 1990), p. 70.]

Appropriate use of humor increases trust in your audience. [W. P. Hampes, "The Relationship Between Humor and Trust," *Humor: International Journal of Humor Research*, 12 (1999): 253–259.]

Humor connects you with your audience and increases their attention to your message. [C. P. Duncan and J. E. Nelson, (1985). "Effects of Humor in a Radio Advertising Experiment," *Journal of Advertising*, 14 (1985): 33–40.]

There is a direct correlation between being charismatic and

having a sense of humor. [Bernard M. Bass, *Bass & Stogdill's Handbook of Leadership*, 3rd ed. (New York: Free Press, 1990), p. 70.]

People are less likely to disagree with you when you use humor. [J. L. Freedman, D. O. Sears, and J. M. Carlsmith, *Social Psychology*, 3rd ed. (Englewood Cliffs, N.J.: Prentice-Hall, 1978).]

SECTION TWO: CORE QUALITIES: INSIDE DICTATES THE OUTSIDE

Chapter 8: Self-Discipline: Willpower Equals Commitment

Talent is not the major cause of success with top athletes, artists, and scholars, it is their extraordinary drive and determination. [Keith Johnson, *The Confidence Makeover: The New and Easy Way to Quickly Change Your Life* (Shippensburg, Penn.: Destiny Image, 2006). A report on a five-year study of 120 of America's top artists, athletes, and scholars, by a team of researchers led by Benjamin Bloom, a University of Chicago education professor.]

Charismatic people emphasize physical and mental toughness, sacrifice, and hard work to overcome hardships and challenges. [R. J. House and J. M. Howell, "Personality and Charismatic Leadership," *Leadership Quarterly*, 3 (1992): 81–108.]

Charismatic people are zealously committed to their mission and their occupation. [R. J. House and J. M. Howell, "Personality and Charismatic Leadership," *Leadership Quarterly*, 3 (1992): 81–108.]

Self-discipline and will power will weaken after doing sequential tasks, much like an overused muscle that has been strained to fatigue or a battery that has lost its charge. [M. Muraven and R. F. Baumeister, "Self-Regulation and Depletion of Limited Resources: Does Self-Control Resemble a Muscle?" *Psychological Bulletin*, 126 (2000): 247–259.]

Chapter 9: Competence: What You Don't Know Can Hurt You

When we don't feel competent or capable it limits our ability to pursue our goals. [http://www.psychologytoday.com/blog/dont-delay/200902/fear-failure]

Feeling competent increases motivation, reduces fear, enhances charisma and leadership. [http://www.psychologytoday.com/blog/dont-delay/200902/fear-failure]

There is a direct correlation between your intelligence and your income. [Kevin Hogan and Mary Lee Labar, *Irresistible Attraction* (Network 3000, 2000).]

There are three primary human needs: for autonomy, for relatedness, and for competence. [Edward Deci and Richard Ryan, *Handbook of Self-Determination Research* (Rochester, NY: University of Rochester Press, 2002).]

There are five critical competencies for today's business:

- Resources: Identifies, organizes, plans, and allocates resources
- Interpersonal: Works with others
- Information: Acquires and evaluates information
- Systems: Understands complex interrelationships
- Technology: Works with a variety of technologies

[U.S. Departments of Labor and Education formed the Secretary's Commission on Achieving Necessary Skills (SCANS) to study the kinds of competencies and skills that workers must have to succeed in today's workplace. The results of the study were published in a document entitled "What Work Requires of Schools: A SCANS Report for America 2000" (http://www.ncrel.org/sdrs/areas/issues/methods/assment/as7scans.htm).]

Chapter 10: Intuition: Follow Your Instinct

College students would watch three 10-second video clips of a professor during their class (beginning, middle, and end) and evaluated the professor on the basis of the professor's warmth, energy, and confidence. The study found that these students' evaluations of the professor were the same as the students that attended the class for the whole semester. [N. Ambady and R. Rosenthal, "Thin Slices of Expressive Behavior as Predictors of Interpersonal Consequences: A Meta-Analysis," *Psychological Bulletin*, 46 (1992): 256–274.]

Top-level managers score higher on using intuition than lower-level managers. [Weston H. Agor (ed.), *Intuition in Organizations: Leading and Managing Productively* (Thousand Oaks, Calif.: Sage Publications, 1989).]

Consciously overanalyzing every situation is very ineffective. [D. Goleman, *Working with Emotional Intelligence* (New York: Bantam Books, 1998).]

Intuition is bigger than we realize. It feeds our expertise, creativity, love, and spirituality. [David G. Myers, "The Powers and Perils of Intuition," November 01, 2002 (http://www.psychologytoday.com/articles/200212/the-powers-and-perils-intuition).]

Chapter 11: Purpose: Tapping into Unlimited Drive

Charismatic managers have a high level of conviction, passion, and commitment about the correctness of their ideas. [Jane Whitney Gibson and Charles W. Blackwell, "Flying High with Herb Kelleher: A Profile in Charismatic Leadership," *Journal of Leadership Studies* (Summer–Fall 1999): 120.]

Charismatic people are dedicated to their vision and are positive they are going in the right direction. [Jane Whitney Gibson and Charles W. Blackwell, "Flying High with Herb Kelleher: A Profile in Charismatic Leadership," *Journal of Leadership Studies* (Summer–Fall 1999): 120; V. E. Frankl, *Man's Search for Meaning: An Introduction to Logotherapy*, 4th ed. (Boston: Beacon Press, 1992), p. 115.]

Victor Frankl says of personal meaning that it "always points, and is directed, to something, someone, other than oneself—be it a meaning to fulfill or another human being to encounter." [As quoted in J. J. Sosik, "The Role of Personal Meaning in Charismatic Leadership," *Journal of Leadership Studies*, 7, 2 (2000): 60–74.]

Purpose is found through altruistic leadership, which is defined as "involves motivation through concern for others." [R. N. Kanungo and M. Mendonca, *Ethical Dimensions of Leadership* (Thousand Oaks, Calif.: Sage Publications, 1996).]

Chapter 12: Integrity: Character Counts

Men rated honesty and integrity as the top two qualities they respect in other men. [*Men's Health* (June 1995).]

Men rated lying/dishonesty as one of the top negative qualities in other men. [*Men's Health* (June 1995).]

People are becoming more tolerant of lying, deception and cheating. [Sharon Begley, "A World of Their Own," *Newsweek* (May 8, 2000): 53–56.]

Employees prefer to work for managers whom they can trust and who are honest with them about the reality of their circumstances. [James C. Sarros, Brian K. Cooper, and Joseph C. Santora, "The Character of Leadership," *Ivey Business Journal Online* (May–June 2007 (company overview). Copyright 2007 University of Western Ontario.]

The studies show 33 percent of people distrust their immediate boss. [John C. Maxwell, *Develop the Leader Within You*, rev. ed. (Nashville: Thomas Nelson, 2000).]

Honesty and integrity were the highest-valued traits in a national survey that asked businessmen and -women to identify the characteristics of superior leaders. ["Ugliness May Trump Charisma, Good Looks in Presidential Leadership," *U.S. Newswire* (August 2007).]

Chapter 13: Courage: Stand Up and Be Counted

Courage is critical to having those uncomfortable conversations and not hiding behind the label of being nice. [I. Barry Goldberg, "Courage (On Leadership)," *Arkansas Business*, 23, 34 (August 28, 2006): 7(1). Copyright 2006 Journal Publishing, Inc.]

The work climate for success is characterized by on equitable reward system that recognizes excellence and by a willingness to take risks and experiment with innovative ideas. [James M. Kouzes and Barry Z. Posner, *The Leadership Challenge*, 4th ed. (San Francisco: Jossey-Bass, 2008), p. 66.]

Courage is one of the main attributes possessed by those who motivate followers to outstanding achievements. [E. F. Borgatta, A. S. Couch, and R. F. Bales, "Some Findings Relevant to the Great Man Theory of Leadership," *American Sociological Review*, 19 (1954): 755–759.]

Courage is integral to the charismatic appeal of leaders such as Moses (leading the Jews out of Egypt), Abraham Lincoln (leading the U.S. through civil war and freeing the slaves), and Martin Luther King, Jr. (advancing civil rights in America). Each of these leaders may have derived personal meaning by courageously facing and overcoming numerous challenges. [E. F. Borgatta, A. S. Couch, and R. F. Bales, "Some Findings Relevant to the Great Man Theory of Leadership," *American Sociological Review*, 19 (1954): 755–759.]

Chapter 14: Creativity: Tap Your Imagination

We are not born creative. We are not creative because our brain is different. We learn creativity. Creativity is not the result of some magic brain region that some people have and others don't. [R. Keith Sawyer, PhD, "Expert: You Too Can Be Creative; It Just Takes Hard Work," *PHYSorg.com* (February 3, 2006) (www.physorg.com/news10540.html).]

As long as you are at least average in your intelligence—you are reading this book so you qualify—you can be creative. [E. P. Torrance, "Creativity Research in Education: Still Alive," in I. A. Taylor and J. W. Getzels (eds.), *Perspectives in Creativity* (Piscataway, N.J.: Transaction Publishers, 1975), pp. 278–296.]

We know that effective leadership is usually based on creative problem solving. [Anthony Middlebrooks, "Teaching Leadership as Creative Problem-Solving," *Academic Exchange Quarterly*, 10, 2 (Summer 2006): 32(6).]

Highly creative people have a high level of specialized knowledge (competence) and are capable of divergent thinking (able to draw on ideas from different disciplines and fields). [Kenneth M. Heilman, MD, Stephen E. Nadeau, MD, and David Q. Beversdorf, MD, "Creative Innovation: Possible Brain Mechanisms," *Neurocase* (2003).]

Chapter 15: Focus: Activity Does Not Equal Accomplishment

A big indicator of success is the ability to control impulses, resist distraction, and stay focused on the task at hand. [*Newsweek* reports approach in New England preschools by psychologist Adele Diamond, "Focus, Not IQ, Might be Best School Skill," Arts & Living, Science & Health.]

A Gallup poll found that workers estimate they waste an average of 1.44 hours a day. [Joseph Carrol, "U.S. Workers Say They Waste About an Hour at Work Each Day," Gallup (September 6, 2007) (www.gallup.com/poll/28618/us-workers-say-they-waste-about-hour-work-each-day.aspx); Chuck Martin, "Executive Skills: How to Improve Your Ability to Focus," *CIO* (November 7, 2006) (www.cio.com/article/26430/Executive_Skills_How_to_Improve_Your_Ability_to_Focus_?page = 1).]

Senior managers and executives say the skill of focus is a personal strength. [Ibid.]

What we eat, how much we sleep, carbonated beverages, whether we eat breakfast, food additives, and refined carbohydrates all affect our ability to concentrate. ["Morning Cereal Can Boost Concentration: UK Study" (http://www.newsmax.com/health/cereal_concentration/2009/04/27/207702.html).]

SECTION THREE: DELIVERY AND COMMUNICATION: SPEAK WITH CONVICTION

Chapter 16: Presentation Skills: Educate, Inspire, and Entertain

Your verbal ability is in direct correlation with the capacity to influence others. [Bernard M. Bass, *Bass & Stogdill's Handbook of Leadership*, 3rd ed. (New York: Free Press, 1990), p. 63.]

The top predictor of professional success and upward mobility is how much you enjoy and how good you are at public speaking. [Tony Alessandra, *Charisma: Seven Keys to Developing the Magnetism That Leads to Success* (New York: Business Plus, 2000).]

The capacity for ready communication is always one of the skills associated with leadership. [Bernard M. Bass, *Bass & Stogdill's Handbook of Leadership*, 3rd ed. (New York: Free Press, 1990).]

The ability to give presentations was ranked as the most critical skill needed to move up in today's business environment. [*American Salesman*, 36, 8 (August 1991): 16(5).]

The majority (75 percent) of executives felt that presentation skills were three times more important than writing skills. [*American Salesman*, 36, 8 (August 1991): 16(5).]

Chapter 17: People Skills: Do They Really Like You?

Studies show that 91 percent of people said people skills are important in business, but 66 percent said their company wasn't committed to developing those skills. ["Damaging Shortage of People Skills," *Personnel Today* (June 18, 2002): 9. Survey says two-thirds of UK companies are not committed to developing people management skills.]

There is an interesting correlation between lawsuits and the likeability of a doctor. Malpractice lawsuit statistics show that patients who feel rushed, treated poorly, or ignored are the most likely to sue their doctors. ["Bulletin: How Plaintiffs' Lawyers Pick Their Targets," *Medical Economics*, 10, 4 (Fall 2001): 47 (http://www.aans .org/library/article.aspx?articleid = 10046).]

The ability to connect with the most people is critical for charisma. Charismatic people were found to be more extroverted in most studies. [Bernard M. Bass, *Bass & Stogdill's Handbook of Leadership*, 3rd ed. (New York: Free Press, 1990), p. 67.]

When CEOs were asked what traits helped them get to the top, the majority said hard work, people skills, and leadership ability. ["What Does It Take to Make It? Sweat, People Skills, Leadership," *American Banker*, 156, 138 (July 19, 1991): 2A(1).]

Chapter 18: Influence: Help Others Persuade Themselves

Great managers possess persuasion skills required to convince others of the quality of their ideas. [Bernard M. Bass, *Bass & Stogdill's Handbook of Leadership*, 3rd ed. (New York: Free Press, 1990).]

When someone persuades you to change your mind, that person will be inclined to be persuaded by you. Conversely, if you resist that person's attempts and do not change your mind, then he or she will likely reciprocate in a similar fashion, resisting your attempts to change his or her mind. [Kurt Mortensen, *Maximum Influence: The 12 Universal Laws of Power Persuasion* (New York: AMACOM, 2004).]

Nonverbal characteristics and behavior are associated with persuasiveness, including vocal pleasantness and facial expressiveness. [J. K. Burgoon, T. Birk, and M. Pfau, "Non-verbal Behaviors,

Persuasion, and Credibility," *Human Communication Resources*, 17 (1990): 140–169.]

Up to 95 percent of persuasion and influence involves a subconscious trigger. This means the inclinations like "It just feels right," "I trust this person," or "I don't like this person" are all based on subconscious emotional reactions. [Joseph Sugarman, Ron Hugher, and Dick Hafer, *Triggers: 30 Sales Tools You Can Use to Control the Mind of Your Prospect to Motivate, Influence and Persuade* (Las Vegas, Nev.: Delstar, 1999).]

Ninety-five percent of thought and emotion occur in the unconscious mind, without our awareness. [Daniel M. Wegner, *The Illusion of Conscious Will* (Cambridge, Mass.: MIT Press, 2002); George Lakoff and Mark Johnson, *Philosophy in the Flesh* (New York: Basic Books, 1999); Antonio Damasio, *The Feeling of What Happens* (New York: Mariner Books, 2000); Gerald Edelman and Giulio Tononi, "Reentry and the Dynamic Core," in Thomas Metzinger (ed.), *Neural Correlates of Consciousness* (Cambridge, Mass.: MIT Press, 2003); Bernard J. Baars, *A Cognitive Theory of Consciousness* (New York: Cambridge University Press, 1988); Joseph LeDoux, *The Emotional Brain* (New York: Simon & Schuster, 1998); John R. Searle, *The Rediscovery of the Mind* (Cambridge, Mass.: MIT Press, 1992); Walter J. Freeman, *How Brains Make Up Their Mind* (New York: Columbia University Press, 2000), pp. 13–36; Steven Pinker, *How the Mind Works* (New York: W.W. Norton, 1997).]

Chapter 19: Storytelling: Create the Image

As human beings, we are drawn to anything that gives us answers. Stories help your audience answer some of their own questions. [Kurt W. Mortensen, *Persuasion IQ: The 10 Skills You Need to Get Exactly What You Want* (New York: AMACOM, 2008).]

Charismatic presidents used nearly twice as many metaphors than noncharismatic presidents. Speeches with metaphors are judged as more inspirational to the audience. [Jeffery Scott Mio, Ronald E. Riggio, Shana Levin, and Renford Reese, *Presidential Leadership and Charisma: The Effects of Metaphor* (California State Polytechnic University, Pomona, Claremont McKenna College, 2005).]

Stories grab attention, create involvement, simplify complex ideas, and persuade without detection. [Kurt W. Mortensen, *Maximum Influence: The 12 Universal Laws of Power Persuasion* (New York: AMACOM, 2004).]

Stories statistically will connect with more people than facts, numbers, examples, or testimonials. [Kurt W. Mortensen, *Persuasion IQ: The 10 Skills You Need to Get Exactly What You Want* (New York: AMACOM, 2008).]

Chapter 20: Eye Contact: Conversing Without Speaking

When you increase appropriate eye contact, people judge you as more dominant, assertive, and independent. [C. L. Brooks, M. A. Church, and L. Fraser, "Effects of Duration of Eye Contact on Judgments of Personality Characteristics," *Journal of Social Psychology*, 126 (1986): 71–78.]

There is a link between the duration of eye contact and the positive judgment of personality characteristics of the requester. [G. Knackstedt and C. Kleinke, "Eye Contact, Gender, and Personality Judgments," *Journal of Social Psychology*, 131 (1191): 303–304.

Good eye contact is judged as having high self-esteem. [J. M. Droney and C. L Brooks, "Attributions of Self-Esteem as a Function of Duration of Eye Contact," *Journal of Social Psychology*, 133 (1993): 715–722.]

Direct eye contact can increase compliance. [C. Kleinke and D. Singer, "Influence of Gaze on Compliance with Demanding and Conciliatory Request in a Field Setting." *Personality and Social Psychology Bulletin*, 5 (1979): 376–390.]

Chapter 21: Listening: Say What?

Studies show that poor listening skills still account for 60 percent of all misunderstandings. [Murray Raphel, "Listening Correctly Can Increase Your Sales," *Direct Marketing*, 41, 11 (November 1982): 113.]

Eighty percent of our success in learning from other people is based on how well we listen. [Marshall Goldsmith and Mark Reiter, *What Got You Here Won't Get You There* (New York: Hyperion, 2007); "Now Go Out and Lead," *BusinessWeek.com* (January 8,

2007) (http://www.businessweek.com/magazine/content/07_02/b40 16083.hm).]

Great managers are great listeners. [*Business Week Online* (February 1, 2007).

We only "hear" because the studies show the average listener expends too much effort on trying to remember the facts. [Eugene Raudsepp, "The Art of Listening Well," *Inc.* (October 1981): 135.]

There is a positive relationship between effective listening and being able to adapt to your audience and persuade them. [S. B. Castleberry and C. D. Shepherd, C.D., "Effective Interpersonal Listening and Personal Selling," *Journal of Personal Selling & Sales Management*, 13 (Winter 1993): 35–49.]

Chapter 22: Rapport: The Instant Connection

When you create a positive perception, you have an 85 percent chance of persuasion. With a negative perception, you have only a 15 percent chance. [Kurt W. Mortensen, *Persuasion IQ: The 10 Skills You Need to Get Exactly What You Want* (New York: AMACOM, 2008).]

A study showed that 75 percent of people don't like all the "gushy, chit-chatty stuff," but 99 percent of them won't even bother to stop you when they're annoyed. [William T. Brooks and Thomas M. Travisano, *You're Working Too Hard to Make the Sale!: More Than 100 Insider Tools to Sell Faster and Easier!* (New York: McGraw-Hill, 1995), p. 47.]

One of the major causes of employees' going into a bad mood was talking to someone in management. [J. Basch and C. D. Fisher, "Affective Events Emotions Matrix: A Classification of Job Related Events and Emotions Experienced in the Workplace," in N. Ashkanasy, W. Zerbe, and C. Hartel (eds.), *Emotions in the Workplace: Research, Theory and Practice* (Westport, Conn.: Quorum Books, 2000), pp. 36–48.]

Our facial muscles (all indicating a different emotion or feeling) can produce over 250,000 different expressions. [R. Birdwhistle, *Kinesics and Context: Essays on Body Motion and Communication* (Philadelphia: University of Pennsylvania Press, 1970).]

SECTION FOUR: EMPOWERING OTHERS: CONTAGIOUS COOPERATION

Chapter 23: Inspiration: Strengthen and Energize

Most American business professionals are uninspired. [Carmine Gallo, "The Seven Secrets of Inspiring Leaders," *Bloomberg BusinessWeek* (October 10, 2007). Carmine Gallo's research reveals techniques common to the leaders who best know how to inspire their employees, investors, and customers.]

Inspirational behavior stimulates enthusiasm among subordinates for the work of the group and builds their confidence in their ability to successfully perform assignments and attain group objectives. [Bernard M. Bass, *Bass & Stogdill's Handbook of Leadership*, 3rd ed. (New York: Free Press, 1990), p. 207.]

Only 10 percent of employees look forward to going to work each day. [Carmine Gallo, "The Seven Secrets of Inspiring Leaders," *Bloomberg BusinessWeek* (October 10, 2007). Carmine Gallo's research reveals techniques common to the leaders who best know how to inspire their employees, investors, and customers.]

Great managers guide and support the personal growth of their supporters and provide intellectual stimulation. [Bernard M. Bass, *Bass & Stogdill's Handbook of Leadership*, 3rd ed. (New York: Free Press, 1990), p. 201.]

Chapter 24: Esteem: Understand the Ego

Self-image is a big aspect of charisma. Self-image encompasses how people describe themselves in terms of needs, beliefs, values, and personal meaning. [W. L. Gardner and B. A. Avolio, "The Charismatic Relationship: A Dramaturgical Perspective," *Academy of Management Review*, 23 (1998): 32–58.]

Praise can also cause people to change their minds. In a study, student essays were randomly given high or low marks. When surveyed, the students who had gotten A's tended to lean even more favorably in the direction of the positions they had advocated in their essays. Students who had received failing marks, however, did not stand behind their previous positions as willingly. [Kurt W.

Mortensen, *Maximum Influence: The 12 Universal Laws of Power Persuasion* (New York: AMACOM, 2004).]

In the first 18 years of life, if you lived in an average home, you were told no or what you could not do more than 148,000 times. [Dr. Shad Helmstetter, "What to Say When You Talk to Yourself," *Pocket* (January 15, 1990): 66.]

Income is a primary reason we work, but most people also want the job satisfaction they get from accomplishment. They have a drive to be part of the team. [R. S. Dreyer, "What It Takes to Be a Leader—Today!" *Supervision*, 55, 5 (May 1994): 22(3).]

Chapter 25: Credibility: Reality Versus Perception

Having success is key to maintaining a charismatic image. [J. A. Conger and R. N. Kanungo, *Charismatic Leadership in Organizations* (Thousand Oaks, Calif.: Sage Publications, 1998).]

Charismatic people are extraordinarily successful. Long-term charisma will always depend on long-term success. [J. A. Conger, and R. N. Kanungo, *Charismatic Leadership in Organizations* (Thousand Oaks, Calif.: Sage Publications, 1998).]

Speech nonfluencies, such as increased pauses, repetitions, and speech errors, have been found to decrease perceptions of credibility. [E. Engstrom, "Effects of Nonfluencies on Speaker's Credibility in Newscast Settings," *Perceptual and Motor Skills*, 83, 2 (1994): 579–588.]

Studies show that people who appear well organized are thought of as being more thorough and better prepared than their disorganized counterparts; this perception, of course, increases their credibility. [Kurt W. Mortensen, *Persuasion IQ: The 10 Skills You Need to Get Exactly What You Want* (New York: AMACOM, 2008).]

Respect is based on the sum total of how you have conducted yourself in your professional and personal affairs. If you have shown respect, integrity, and character in all your dealings, people will know it. People will sense it. [Kurt W. Mortensen, *Persuasion IQ: The 10 Skills You Need to Get Exactly What You Want* (New York: AMACOM, 2008).]

Chapter 26: Motivation: Light Their Fire

A study shows 59 percent said their companies do not do enough to motivate employees. [B. Reece and R. Brandt, *Effective Human Relations in Organizations*, 2nd ed. (Englewood Cliffs, N.J.: Prentice-Hall, 1982).]

Over 50 percent of all workers say they could double their effectiveness, and 85 percent of workers in the U.S said they could work harder on the job. [F. Herzberg, *The Motivation to Work* (New York: John Wiley & Sons, 1959).]

Dr. W. Edwards Deming says the way to high productivity is to move staff toward intrinsic motivation, having the capability and authority to bring about change in their sphere of influence. [W. E. Deming, "A System of Profound Knowledge," participant material distributed at the Quality Seminar (March 1991), Santa Clara, California.]

The process of moving toward a desired change is equally as rewarding as the end result. [Victor Vroom, *Work and Motivation* (San Francisco: Jossey-Bass, 1994).]

Only 42 percent feel managers use top motivating techniques. [B. Reece and R. Brandt, *Effective Human Relations in Organizations*, 2nd ed. (Englewood Cliffs, N.J.: Prentice-Hall, 1982).]

Chapter 27: Goodwill: Charity and Compassion

Helping others not only builds self-respect, but also improves your health. People who do volunteer work and care for others have a 60 percent lower rate of premature death. [Robin Koval and Linda Kaplan Thaler, *The Power of Nice: How to Conquer the Business World with Kindness* (New York: Broadway Business, 2006), p. 104.]

Showing concern means exhibiting genuine friendliness and goodwill for the other person's best interest. It means acting with consideration, politeness, and civility. It is the foundation for all interactions, and it creates an environment of concern in return. [Kurt W. Mortensen, *Persuasion IQ: The 10 Skills You Need to Get Exactly What You Want* (New York: AMACOM, 2008).]

Our society places great value on charisma. If you happen to be charismatic, great, but that isn't the signature characteristic of a great leader. We think kindness is. [William F. Baker, *Leading with Kindness: How Good People Consistently Get Superior Results* (New York: AMACOM, 2008).]

Employees should be involved in organizational plans and changes. They should be treated as individuals because in return they will perform better and be satisfied in their jobs. [R. S. Dreyer, "What It Takes to Be a Leader—Today!" *Supervision*, 55, 5 (May 1994): 22(3).]

Chapter 28: Vision: See It, Taste It, Touch It, Feel It

When you need to express a vision, get buy-in, and implement it. That calls for open, caring relations with employees and face-to-face communication. People who cannot convincingly articulate a vision won't be successful. [N. M. Tichy and S. Sherman, *Control Your Own Destiny or Someone Else Will* (New York: HarperBusiness, 1994).]

More than one-third (36 percent) surveyed value a visionary people person for their leader. ["Ugliness May Trump Charisma, Good Looks in Presidential Leadership Test" (http://www.alma.edu/academics/leadership/leadership_survey); copyright 2007 PR Newswire Association LLC.]

Charismatic people are "meaning makers" who "interpret reality to offer us images of the future that are irresistible. [J. A. Conger, *The Charismatic Leadership: Behind the Mystique of Exceptional Leadership* (San Francisco: Jossey-Bass, 1989).]

Meaning is important for follower identification with the person and his or her vision. [J. A. Conger and R. N. Kanungo, *Charismatic Leadership in Organizations* (Thousand Oaks, Calif.: Sage Publications, 1998).]

Managers who clearly articulate a vision found higher levels of job satisfaction, motivation, commitment, pride in the organization, and organizational productivity. [James M. Kouzes and Barry Z. Posner, *The Leadership Challenge*, 4th ed. (San Francisco: Jossey-Bass, 2008), p. 124.]

Chapter 29: Empathy: Compassion Creates Friendship

Executives rated the skills expected of business managers (business aptitude, responsibility, clarity, self-confidence, etc.), but the qualities that best predicted high ratings for effectiveness—what mattered most to their colleagues—were empathy and trustworthiness. ["Empathy Matters Most for Effective Leadership," BlessingWhite (December 26, 2007) (http://www.blessingwhite.com/docDescription.asp?id=216&pid=6&sid=1).]

Charismatic people have a strong tendency to display sensitivity toward people's needs and emotions. [J. A. Conger and R. N. Kanungo, *Charismatic Leadership in Organizations* (Thousand Oaks, Calif.: Sage Publications, 1998).]

Great managers share followers' feelings in a way that creates an emotional bond between them. [P. Salovey and J. D. Mayer, "Emotional Intelligence," *Imagination, Cognition and Personality*, 9 (1990): 185–211.]

Charismatic people pay individualized attention to followers, respond to their needs, and encourage their personal development. [B. M. Bass, *Leadership and Performance Beyond Expectations* (New York: Free Press, 1985).]

Charismatic managers respect followers and are concerned about their feelings and needs. [P. M. Podsakoff, S. B. MacKenzie, R. H. Moorman, and R. Fetter, "Transformational Leader Behaviors and Their Effects on Followers' Trust in Leader, Satisfaction, and Organizational Citizenship Behaviors," *Leadership Quarterly*, 1 (1990): 107–142.]

Want charisma? The best predictors are empathy and trustworthiness. [*WFC Resources Newsbrief* (February 2008), 5, 2.]

Chapter 30: Respect: Give It to Get It

Respect is critical to the organization. Companies that value "pro-people practices" tend to perform up to 40 percent better over time. These organizations have cultures that have continuous learning, teamwork, and concern for all key stakeholders. [R. Brayton Bowen, "Today's Workforce Requires New Age Currency: Responsibility, Respect, Relationships, Recognition and Rewards Work Well Together to Motivate Workers," *HR Magazine* (March 2004).]

Managers know that good manners are important to success in workplace relationships. Good manners also enhance team performance, in listening and responding to customers, and in managing a richly diverse workforce. [Frances Hesselbein, "The Power of Civility: Demonstrate Appreciation and Respect," *The Non-profit Times*, 16, 21 (November 1, 2002): 48(2).]

Absenteeism is up in U.S. workplaces, and there is a direct association with absenteeism and employee morale. Nearly twice as many companies with "poor/fair" morale reported an increase in unscheduled absences over the past two years compared to companies with "good/very good" morale (33 percent versus 17 percent). Moreover, 46 percent of companies with low morale reported that unscheduled absenteeism is a serious problem for them. ["Employers Still Struggle with High Cost of Absenteeism," *HR.com* (October 28, 2001) (http://www.hr.com/SITEFORUM?&t = /Default/gateway &i = 1116423256281&application = story&active = no&ParentID = 1119278060936&StoryID = 1119648002296&xref = http%3A//www .google.com/search%3Fhl%3Den%26q%3DCCH + HR + Management + absent eeism%26aq%3Df%26oq%3D%26aqi%3D).]

When people were polled to see what aspect of trust they thought was most important, 44 percent said credibility. Interestingly, despite its importance, respondents felt it was established only 11.4 percent of the time. [Kurt W. Mortensen, *Persuasion IQ: The 10 Skills You Need to Get Exactly What You Want* (New York: AMACOM, 2008).]

INDEX